Living Well as a Single Mom

Cynthia Yates

HARVEST HOUSE PUBLISHERS
EUGENE, OREGON

SEP 07

Cover photos © William McKellar / Brand X Pictures / Alamy; BananaStock / Alamy; Ron Chapple / Thinkstock / Alamy; Holidays and Celebrations / Stockdisc

Cover by Terry Dugan Design, Minneapolis, Minnesota

Cynthia Yates: Published in association with the literary agency of Janet Kobobel Grant, Books & Such, 4788 Carissa Avenue, Santa Rosa, California 95405

Backcover author photo © Janis Krause

LIVING WELL AS A SINGLE MOM
Copyright © 2006 by Cynthia Yates
Published by Harvest House Publishers
Eugene, Oregon 97402
www.harvesthousepublishers.com
Library of Congress Cataloging-in-Publication Data

Yates, Cynthia, 1947–
Living well as a single mom / Cynthia Yates.
   p. cm.
ISBN-13: 978-0-7369-1651-6
ISBN-10: 0-7369-1651-2
1. Single mothers—Religious life. I. Title.
BV4529.18.Y38 2006
248.8'431—dc22   2005020522

Printed in the United States of America

06 07 08 09 10 11 12 13 14 / BP-MS / 10 9 8 7 6 5 4 3 2 1

I dedicate this book to you, single mom,
and countless women like you who have
persevered and raised great kids.

Acknowledgments

I offer gratitude and thanks to the single mothers who contributed to this work.

I thank Wonder Man (my husband, Joe) for his endurance, my agent and friend Janet Kobobel Grant, my editor and friend Gene Skinner, and the staff of Harvest House Publishers.

Contents

A Note from the Author

Two of my previous books would make excellent adjuncts to *Living Well as a Single Mom*. They are *Living Well on One Income* and *Ditch the Diet and the Budget*. Each represents a unique way to achieve my goal: to help you. Taken together, they offer extensive skills, tips, and philosophies to improve your circumstance and to help you live well according to God's purpose for your life.

This book contains some redundancies because I believe we learn more effectively through repetition. For example, I address TV viewing in more than one chapter.

My passion on certain issues spills onto the page not as rebuke but as a verbal exclamation point to make my concern clear. I am 100 percent on your side. In fact, that's what this book is all about: your side of the story and getting you through this profound responsibility of raising children to God.

I am sensitive about time constraints. Rather than asking you to flip to an appendix for additional sources, I have included a resource list and reading list at the end of most chapters.

One

The Many Faces
of Single Mothers

Brookies Cookies is to Bigfork, Montana, what the Empire State Building is to New York City, the Golden Gate is to San Francisco, and the Arch is to St. Louis. Whoever you are, when you are in Bigfork, you go to Brookies and you buy a cookie.

Besides being a local landmark, Brookies is a place where locals congregate. It is also a place where I commandeer a corner table and work when a change of scenery helps my creativity. On one such occasion I had the following conversation with another of the regulars.

"What are you working on now, Cynthia?"

"A book to help the single mom."

(Derisive snort.) "I met one yesterday."

"Oh?"

"She was a bell ringer for the Salvation Army. I asked her if she got paid for ringing the bell. She said she did, said she needed the money to support her six kids." (Enough snorts to get a Snickerdoodle caught in his sinus cavity.) "I walked away in disgust. I mean, she got herself pregnant six times."

And so the stereotype goes. According to that fellow, the woman was a blight on society and most certainly a drain on our social services. Further conversation with the man made his position clear: In his eyes the woman represented one of the many things wrong with this country, by golly. The hapless mom on the sidewalk must be weak, uncivilized, too ignorant to keep her legs crossed at the ankles, or worse, milking the system. If you ask me, he failed to notice one rather remarkable accomplishment, something that should warrant profound amazement—she got pregnant all by herself six times! Right. And pigs fly.

I don't know if you have one child or six—or sixteen for that matter. And, frankly, I'm not going to put too much energy into the reasons why. We will look at the many faces of single mothers, but why and how you became one is not my main concern. My objective is to help you to live your life as a single mom and to live it well. I am going to do that by helping you get through today. That's all. "Today" is where I will invest most of my energy and where you should too because in case you haven't noticed, there's a lot of work to do.

Tomorrow Never Comes

Face it! In spite of the emotional stew you may be marinating in, in spite of the big, overwhelming picture of getting your kids through childhood in one piece (and in reasonable mental, physical, and emotional health); in spite of the bills, the loneliness, the laundry, the cranky car transmission; in spite of your boss, your mother, and your ex; your colossal challenge is to get through today. Tomorrow is soon enough to cope with those matters, and cope with them you will, but your path to tomorrow goes smack through today. My question to you is this: Do you want to stand on tomorrow's doorstep with both feet

Today is the tomorrow you worried about yesterday.

planted, hands on your hips, and a bring-it-on glint in your eye? You can. Let today reign. Make the steps of today matter, and let tomorrow take care of itself.

Has it occurred to you that tomorrow never comes? You can catch a cold, you can catch a bus, but you can't catch tomorrow. It will always be ahead of you, teasing or threatening, just out of reach until you finally get close enough…to grab nothing but a fistfull of air. Tomorrow vaporizes as quickly as it begins. You go through the door and *presto!* you're right back into today. Let me help you to live for this day, not in a careless manner, ignoring the weightier needs of your future or of sound plans, but in the way and words of the Master. Jesus said, "Do not worry about tomorrow, for tomorrow will worry about itself. Each day has enough trouble of its own" (Matthew 6:34).

Living Well as a Single Mom

Living well—regardless of who you are—is a critical testimony to a watching world. Besides, who wouldn't want to live well? *Sign me up, Cynthia, and show me how!* Great—the first step is to understand what I mean by "living well." If you've read previous books of mine, you already know that by living well I mean living according to God's purpose for your life, understanding that He is in control regardless of your circumstance, and finding joy in that understanding. Joy even in the face of adversity.

Wait a second! Are you telling me that God's purpose for my life is to be alone? To have suffered loss? To be stuck in a rut so deep I'm wallowing in muck and gasping for air? To run myself ragged while dealing with snotty noses, snotty children, and snotty feelings that grip me by the throat and shake me till I lose any sense of worth or equilibrium? This is His plan for my life?! Forgetaboutit!

I don't know. I'd need a Doctor of Divinity degree to figure all that out. We'd have to consider the matter of free will, of sin, of straying from His original plan for your life. By the time I found myself a single mom, I'd messed up plenty and had never given God's plan for my life the time of day. (Or my own plan. Didn't have one.) I didn't even believe in God much when I was first homeless with a young child. (That's right—homeless.) Though those were hard years for me to live through, I look back and see redemptive grace working in my life *in spite* of my skepticism and rebellion. I have learned that regardless of our circumstances or how we got in them, God still has a plan for our lives. Foremost in that plan is our relationship with Him, followed by bearing His image to a hurting world. Next in His plan is a no-brainer: He gave you a life so you could live it—and live it well.

Bringing God into the picture is necessary because I do not believe you can succeed in the natural world without the spiritual. I am holistic and cover a lot of bases in my books, ever aware of body, mind, and spirit. How can anyone live well by ignoring one-third of who she is? I am aware that many women eschew anything religious, sometimes for good reason. Some women have suffered at the hands of supposedly religious people, including their husbands. But that doesn't change the importance of attending to your personal relationship with God one bit.

Certainly living well includes more than living according to God's purpose for your life in a spiritual sense. Living well also means *having* a life: paying the bills, eating healthy meals, living in healthy bodies, and keeping a relatively happy and harmonious home—with children. We have a lot of ground to cover, so let's get down to business by looking into the many faces of the single mom.

As I begin, let me get something straight: I did not live well as a single mom. I survived. I survived through sheer grit, dumb luck, the grace of God, and the kindness of strangers. I eked out a living, but I didn't fare so well emotionally, physically, socially, or spiritually. (Picture me rocking in a fetal position on my kitchen floor and drooling.) Though I seemed to be holding it all together on the outside, I was a mess on the inside.

I want to get something else straight: My stint as a single mom lasted less than two years, barely giving me enough experience to weigh in on this issue, though those were profoundly difficult times for my son and me.

My time as a *virtual* single mom, however, spanned from the birth of my son through his seventh year. My years as the daughter of a virtual single mom spanned my entire childhood.

"Virtual?" asked my friend Holly. "I've never heard of a virtual single mom."

"Just made it up."

"Oh."

"You see, Holly," I continued, "a whole lot of women are single moms in spite of being married."

"Yeah, like who?" asked Holly.

"Well, like women whose husbands are in the military. Or in prison. Or ill. Or never home. Or emotionally absent. Women married to those men are virtual single moms."

"Ah…there are a lot more single moms than I thought."

Who Is the Single Mom?

There *are* a whole lot more single moms than any of us thought. Until now, just like Holly, many of us think of single moms as women who are alone through divorce, death, abandonment, choice, or family circumstance. (Roughly ten million strong, according to government statistics.)[1] But that's only part of the picture.

I'd wager that ten million can be easily doubled to reflect the virtual as well as the actual single mothers out there. That's a lot of millions. Who are all these women? A cursory glance at my family and some friends gives us an inkling:

- I was a single mom through divorce. But prior to divorce, I was a virtual single mom due to a husband who could not emotionally grasp the full responsibility of being a husband and father. I was mother and father to my son.

- My own father could not cope with marital or parental responsibility and seemed only to be able to tend to himself. My two sisters and I were raised by a virtual single mom.

- My mother's mother, direct from Poland, raised five children in spite of my Polish grandfather's inability to cope with life. Beaten by the Russians and left for dead, my grandfather's spirit was dashed to smithereens long before he immigrated to America. My "Babci" was a virtual single mom.

- The exacting demands of graduate school kept our grown son marginally distanced from his family until he received his doctorate. At times this put pressure on our daughter-in-law to persevere as a virtual single mom.

- A friend suffers from multiple sclerosis, another from the ravages of alcoholism, another from a brain injury. The wives of these three men have been forced to act as single moms to their respective children.

- One young friend bears the responsibility of small children as her husband serves in the military. Another friend raised children while her husband spent months on submarine duty. One friend had to cope with her husband's debilitating depression after he returned from Vietnam.

- One friend's father checked out emotionally because of his inability to cope with the demands of a mentally challenged child.

I could extend this list indefinitely; these are a sample from my immediate family and friends. For an example of an "actual" single mom, my mother-in-law lost her husband to a drunk driver when her son, who would later become my husband, was five years old.

Actual or virtual, single moms are everywhere. The U.S. Census Bureau claims that 61 percent of all children will spend some time in a single-parent household, most of those households run by women.[2] This statistic is an eye-opener. How and why did this happen?

The Faces of Actual Single Mothers: The Divorced Mom

About half of all marriages end in divorce. That includes marriages blessed through religious ceremonies. (I've read that the only group of couples that show a marked improvement are those who pray together.) The preponderance of marriages that end in divorce have produced children. Shazam—single moms. A lot of them.

Divorce can come as a result of prolonged strife, it can come from out of the blue, and sometimes it can come as a colossal relief. Is divorce sometimes necessary? Unequivocally, yes. Especially as a result of unrepentant infidelity (including pornography), threat to the family through crime or addiction, or abuse. (In my estimation, some other versions of abuse are as destructive and painful as physical abuse.)

It happens often: A hapless, worn-down, desperate mother struggles to keep the family together while a derelict or emotionally unfit father runs his family into the ground before he runs off (or is carted off by the law). And who is left with the mess? Mom. What happens next? Sometimes the woman is vilified, often she is shunned or abandoned, and routinely she is overlooked by those who should be rushing to her aid.

It happens often: A wife is living her dream, maybe with a tiny intuitive pull in her spirit that something is amiss, when one perfectly normal day the announcement comes. "I don't love you anymore. I've found someone else. I need to get on with my life, and you don't fit in my plans." Thunderstruck, she staggers like a zombie through the system: property division, child support, visitation rights, papers to sign, anniversary dates to face, children to raise, lunches to make, snow tires to put on, electric bills to pay. Sometimes she clings stubbornly to illusions of reuniting and will not—cannot—let go.

It happens often: A wife wants out of the marriage. Freedom, fulfillment, lack of love or intimacy, new horizons—whatever the reason, the husband is sometimes blindsided by a wife who calls it quits and takes the children with her.

It happens often: Relationships hit tilt. All the counseling in the world is not going to redeem two hearts that are polarized with rancor and strife. You just want out; he just wants out. The kids will just have to adjust.

What About the Kids?

"It's better for the kids," you convince yourselves. "Anything would be better than for them to be exposed to such stress and animosity." You may be right. I heard one TV psychologist state that kids would rather be from a broken home than live in one. Maybe yes, maybe no. I'd rather put it this way: Children may be from a broken family (in the traditional sense), but they never need to be from a broken home.

I've spoken to children who welcomed peace into their homes and were glad their father was out of the picture. Did they long for a father deep down? "Well sure, but not the way it was. Maybe—you know—a real dad, or parents who got along…family…everybody a family." Conversations became wistful and eyes tended to drift away at that point.

I've also spoken to kids who were positively devastated by divorce and missed their fathers desperately regardless of the visitation arrangements.

And I've spoken to kids who have settled into divorce with a shrug because it is commonplace.

Marital breakup is built into our culture as one of many reasonable life-affirming options. Divorce is so mainstream that our six-year-old granddaughter—who lives in a secure family environment—engaged me in a telling conversation:

"Gram, if you and Pop ever split up…"

"Gram and Pop will never split up, Ellen."

"Oh, Gram, you never know!"

An Appeal

I feel compelled to make an appeal for reconsideration in your decision for divorce.

Do I feel marriages should stay intact because of the children? One young man I spoke to thought they should. One older teen told me he felt valued because his parents chose the hard task of staying together for his sake. I've spoken to kids who recognized the supreme sacrifice their "warring" parents were making by trying to stay together.

Children ideally need both a mother and a father in a safe and nurturing family environment under one roof. (Key words: "safe and nurturing.") Slow down if you are in the throes of divorce. Don't be too quick to terminate solely on individual rights that supersede the rights of your family. We have become nearly hysterical with traditional-family phobia in our earnest desire to uphold individual rights over any inkling of responsibility to a greater cause. Family is our most basic and fundamental social structure. I believe it was the essayist Wendell Barry who wrote that families live on compromise, sacrifice, kindness, love, fortitude, goodwill, and growth. These attributes are also necessary in the greater social cause—the families we call our neighborhood, our town, our country, and our planet Earth.

When I speak of a traditional family, I speak ideally of a mom, a dad, and kids. Because some bad characters and wrong thinking entered the family dynamic, bad press and phobia have sprung up toward what many postulate as ideal. Some women have suffered, trying to hold together a traditional family. This suffering continues as millions of virtual single mothers carry the burden of household management or child rearing, at times because of the husband and father's dereliction. This in no way discredits the value of both mother *and* father in the healthy development of children. Those who claim Christ should be vanguards in establishing healthy models through behavior rather than through rhetoric. We scream that we want traditional families, yet we fail to follow the biblical precepts of self-sacrifice, respect, and unconditional love. Family is too important for cheap sloganeering. It is the most important thing we have.

I'm not going to weigh in on the argument of what makes a modern family, nor would I suggest that women must have a man in order to be complete or for their hardships to be over. When I was a child, my family was essentially matriarchal. Your family right now is matriarchal by virtue of your single-parent position. Yet any way you look at it, family is vital to the furthering of society. We learn to function within society first by how we navigate our family environment. Lessons should come from sound and healthy modeling by both parents.

Crucial counsel: If you or your children are in danger in any manner, you must find refuge. No one, under any circumstance, has the right to abuse you or your children.

These days we bring not only dysfunctional backgrounds into marriages but also a checklist of unmet needs. Hand in hand with dysfunction and unmet needs comes the constant cultural mandate to "love and fulfill ourselves." I am first in line to campaign for strong self-worth, but I worry that we can easily misappropriate exhortations to "love thyself." When we fall for "self above everything else" propaganda, our fulfillment might be accomplished at someone's expense. In a family, that someone can be the three-year-old who finally learned to hold a fork and not eat Jell-O and whipped cream with his mitts anymore.

Can the virtue of strong family be modeled within a single-parent household? Of course it can.

Let me shout from the rooftops for those of you who are divorced and raising children on your own: I am a realist; I am on your side. I intend to do my utmost to get others on your side too, if only by awareness of your plight, your fears, your loneliness, your unmet needs as a woman, and your desire to do a superb job of raising your children.

More Faces of Actual Single Moms

The Widowed Mom

I cannot begin to understand what the death of a husband does to a woman's heart. I can guess, I can approximate, but I cannot begin to know your pain. Or your anger. To have your lover ripped from you …especially now, when the children are still young or at home, can only feel wrong and cruel—even if death seemed a merciful end to suffering. You are alone, and your bed is empty. I'm sorry.

On top of this insurmountable loss, you may be denied your rightful expression of grief. The children need baths, meals, discipline, new shoes. They need your strength and support in order to face their father's death. They need hugs, piano lessons, and T-ball. They *need*. How will you manage to meet their needs? Let me tell you this with confidence: You will.

The Abandoned Mother

He found out you were pregnant and that was the last you saw of him. Or he rejected you and your child outright. Maybe you thought the baby would bring him around, stir some fatherly responsibility or duty, or cause him to recognize how much he really wants you. And now he's completely out of the picture.

Or you found yourself pregnant and kept your child. You never, ever planned it this way. And here you are: alone. Well, not exactly alone. You have your child…or children. And you may still be a child yourself, or barely into adulthood. Regardless of your age or your circumstance, you find yourself abandoned. Life may be upside-down, inside out. Maybe you even want out. What do you do? What you do is pick yourself up and get on your feet. Then you put those feet one in front of the other and head down the road to motherhood. If you like, I'll walk with you.

The Single Mom by Choice

Some women parent alone by choice. Altruism, life experience, distrust of marriage, biological clocks, and not having met a soul mate are some reasons women go it alone. Many women have sacrificially taken foster children into their homes and have adopted older children and babies alike. This is a worthy purpose for life.

On the other hand, to have a child for the sake of completing one's self, or as a necessary accessory, would not be on my list of noble and purposeful endeavors. I read the work of one person who made the choice to be a single mom sound like blissful self-realization and regarded fatherhood as archaic, oppressive, and clearly unnecessary. Needless to say, that author and I are not in agreement. In my opinion, the role of a father or of a healthy male role model cannot be overstated. Chapter 3 will expand on this.

The Single Mom Not by Choice

I interviewed one woman for this book who brings a totally different perspective to single mothering: rape. Date-raped at 16, she conceived and bore her first child. Her courageous choice to use this experience to create awareness of date rape and pregnancy does not diminish the fact that she had emotions to confront and became a mom at a tender age. Though not originally by choice—and because of a violent crime against her—this young woman has become another in the ranks of single moms, one who cares for her child with utmost love and dedication.

The Grandmother as a Single Mother

Reasons abound why grandmothers suddenly find themselves at the helm again. According to the Census Bureau, 2.4 million grandparents have the primary responsibility for their grandchildren.[3] My hope is that this book will act as a refresher and an update for those women who have welcomed a new brood into their arms in mid to later life.

The Faces of Virtual Single Mothers

Let's pull the drapes back and take a closer look inside some seemingly intact and functioning families.

The Caregiver Mother

Your husband is ill. This puts you in the position of caregiver *and* virtual single mom. Managing the care of someone who is disabled or sick while meeting the demands of parenting is a huge task. Perhaps the father can still play a viable relational role with the children and even provide some help, if only to share responsibilities in spirit. This situation is a double-whammy. While you take "in sickness and in health" seriously and would not dream of complaining, yours is a very full plate.

The Military and Law Enforcement Mother

At this writing we are at war. With or without war, many women find themselves virtual single mothers as husbands are called to military duty. One small solace in this arrangement is the network of other mothers with whom to share child-rearing issues, other women who understand the knot in your gut as you count the days for your husband's tour to be over. Another consolation is that, as one military wife put it, many of these women knew what they were getting into. One not-so comforting fact is that divorce rates spike when spouses go off to war.[4]

Wives of military personnel, law enforcement officers, and firefighters share a dubious distinction: Their husbands are in the line of fire. The phone might ring, and a grim stranger may appear at your door. This concern weighs heavily as you do your best to create a normal, happy environment for your children.

The Prison Mother

It happens. Men go to prison. The stigma of divorce has dramatically diminished, but the stigma of your children's father being in jail is another matter. Women are often secondary victims of their husband's crime as they are suddenly left holding the bag (which is usually empty). These are big hurdles to jump: making a positive environment for your children, offsetting any negative modeling that may have come from the father, and holding your head high while you try to get by.

The Academic, Professional, or Pastoral Mother

Does any wife of a PhD candidate or medical resident in the world not feel like a virtual single mother at times? Or the wife of a man who spends untold hours away from home by virtue of his occupation? (Worthy of mention are the wives of pastors who bear up under constant interruption to their family routine and who live in a fishbowl.) At issue is the unrelenting monster that grips your husband and wrings him dry as it demands more and more time and energy. The decision to power through for the degree or to stay the course with the job is mutual and for a season. Regardless, mom is still in charge, virtually caring for the day-to-day routine by herself. We need some sort of honorary title for women who selflessly work toward the same goals as their husbands. Parenting solo is no less hard for them.

Emotionally Distant

I have firsthand experience as a daughter of a virtual single mom and as a virtual single mom myself. I married a man similar to my father, who lacked the ability or interest to involve himself in parenting. As a restaurant worker, my dad was often gone, his work taking him away from our home every evening, his dalliances often keeping him away all night. We children quickly learned the discipline of silence when he was home lest we wake the sleeping man who smelled like a deep-fat fryer. In my case, my first husband also was not able to participate in meaningful parenting.

Many women are married to men who live within the same walls and provide financially but have removed themselves from the family emotionally or conversationally. Whether glued to an easy chair and the ball game, out fishing, playing golf, or on the Internet and the like, these men do not involve themselves in either their marriage or their children, leaving the mother a virtual single parent in a two-parent home. The wife and mother finds herself in a profoundly lonely situation.

Which face am I?

How did this happen?

What three main emotions do I feel about how this happened?

Which of those emotions aren't helping me one bit?

How do I feel about my children?

Do my children know how I feel about them?

Is mothering the main purpose of my life right now?

You Know Who You Are: Why Does It Matter?

I wanted to put a face on each type of single mom. (If I left you out, this book is for you too!) Above all else, I wanted you to understand that you are not alone because many mothers have walked before you, walk next to you, and share your circumstance. I have tracked down women just like you and interviewed them because I wanted their voices—voices like yours—to be heard.

Whether you are divorced, you are a single mom by choice, or your husband is in jail, all I want to do is help you. As I said before, you have work to do—the most important work you will ever face and most likely the hardest work you will ever face: You have children to raise.

Another reason I identified different types of single moms is this: In order to understand yourself today, you must understand that you are as much your past as you are your future. Getting in touch with your past will help you be fully present now and experience more of what God has in mind for your future.

To be sure, single mothers live, work, struggle, and succeed *in the now*. Each day brings enough to keep you busy, each buzz of the dryer brings enough laundry, each little emergency and tearful face brings enough drama, each visit from the mailman brings enough bills.

But recognizing how you got to now, how you formed your worldview, how you think about life, and how you look at your circumstances all has to do with what you have experienced before. That is why I wanted you to take a peek at who you are. Unless your husband's sudden death thrust the role of single parent upon you, chances are that you have plenty of background that brought you to where you are.

Think about this: Some women have cluttered homes. Curiously, much clutter is old stuff that no longer serves purpose. The same can be said of hearts. At times, much of the clutter in broken hearts comes from old stuff (jumbled thoughts, dashed hopes, lost relationships, and other life experiences) that no longer serves any purpose. How does a room look once clutter is removed? The very appearance of an uncluttered room causes the spirit to soar. What if a cluttered heart was swept clean and renewed?

> Create in me a clean heart, O God, and put a new and right
> spirit within me. Cast me not away from thy presence, and
> take not thy holy Spirit from me. Restore to me the joy of

thy salvation, and uphold me with a willing spirit (Psalm 51:10-12 RSV).

Meet Marcie

I've interviewed many single mothers and integrated their comments into this book. One particular voice stands alone—Marcie's.

Marcie is a composite woman. Her quotes represent verbatim statements as well as shorthand versions of the feelings or struggles of the mothers I encountered. I use Marcie for a little sass, a little humor, and a whole lot of honest sentiment.

——————————— RESOURCES ———————————

Church Initiative, headquartered in Wake Forest, North Carolina, was founded by Steve and Cheryl Grissom. It is a nondenominational, nonprofit ministry that equips local churches to help people recover from life crises. A phone call or a visit to their website may lead you to an active group near you. (1-800-489-7778 [US and Canada], 919-562-2114 [local and international], info@churchinitiative.org, www.churchinitiative.org) I highly recommend you consider one of their excellent programs:

> DivorceCare is a seminar and small group resource designed to help churches to effectively minister to people who are hurting because of separation and divorce. (www.divorcecare.org)
>
> DivorceCare for Kids is designed to bring healing to children of divorce and to give them hope and the tools to develop healthier relationships within their own families. (www.DC4K.org)
>
> Before You Divorce is a ministry strategy to help save failing marriages. (www.beforeyoudivorce.org)
>
> GriefShare is an innovative resource to assist churches in offering effective ongoing ministry to those who are grieving the loss of a loved one. (www.griefshare.org)

National Domestic Violence Hotline offers crisis intervention, information about domestic violence, and referrals to local service providers through qualified hotline advocates who offer help in English and Spanish. Hotline advocates have access to translators in 139 languages. (1-800-799-7233, TTY: 1-800-787-3224, www.ndvh@ndvh.org)

Single Moms on a Mission is an organization with a mission to improve the quality of life for single parents and their children by providing resources to strengthen the emotional, spiritual, and financial state of the one-parent family. (www.singlemoms.org)

Focus on the Family offers an endless assortment of books and resources to help mothers cope in nearly every aspect of life. (www.family.org)

Pastor's Wives' Support Board is a Web page sponsored by Rock Dove Publications. It is filled with helpful suggestions, advice, support, and encouragement from other women who are pastors' wives. (www.rockdove.com/pw21.html)

Grandparents Rights Organization is a national volunteer nonprofit organization that educates and supports grandparents and grandchildren, and advocates their desire to continue a relationship threatened with loss of contact. Though not specifically intended for grandmothers who have custody of children, its newsletters may be of help. (www.grandparentsrights.org)

Visit the **Military Wives** website (www.militarywives.com) and click on the branch of the Armed Forces that applies to you. These sites are filled with data and information from daily inspiration to craft ideas. A monthly e-newsletter is available.

READING

Kari West and Noelle Quinn, *When He Leaves: Help and Hope for Hurting Wives* (Eugene, OR: Harvest House Publishers, 2005). Includes information on the issues of infidelity and pornography.

Tricia Goyer, *A Life Interrupted: The Scoop on Being a Young Mom* (Grand Rapids, MI: Zondervan Publishing, 2004).

Rick Warren, *The Purpose-Driven Life* (Grand Rapids, MI: Zondervan Publishing, 2002).

Two

Coping

"Earth to you: You already are coping."

Marcie

Being a single mom is certainly the most important thing you will ever do, and in spite of its rewards and magic moments, it isn't easy. Child rearing is hard work. Yet this book is not just about child rearing. It's about you. It's about how you can live well as a single mom, even though it's all about the kids. Does that sound convoluted? Single motherhood presents you with a conundrum: Should your life be about you or the kids?

Yes.

This is a "chicken or the egg" paradox. Right now, for this season in your life, it's all about the kids. But to get to the kids, we have to get through you. You are their shield, their provider, their comfort, their storyteller, their chauffeur, their chief, their cook and bottle washer. Therefore, it's all about you too.

Let me put it this way: You're on an airplane with your young child. The plane goes into a spin. (No, it doesn't crash.) Oxygen masks drop down in front of you. Who do the attendants say you should put a mask on first? Yourself or your child?

You must understand that you are more than the sum total of your efforts as a single mom. You are a vital, engaging, interesting, and talented woman with opinions, emotions, skills, education, sensitivities, needs, and desires. You are contributing both as a mother and as a player in the world around you.

During this time of active motherhood, you have specific, primary goals: to raise relatively stable and healthy children in a safe environment, to prepare them adequately for the complexities of life, and to provide a solid model for your children to emulate. In order to do this you need to care for your body, mind, and spirit, and you need to order your world. To give your kids the care and guidance they need, you have to pay attention to yourself.

Before you can give all this attention, you learn to cope. And to do that, you might consider examining how you behave when you *don't* cope: What pushes your buttons and what derails you? What does your attitude say about you as a vital human being who also happens to be a single mom? You know—the person who has to get up every morning, sick or healthy, to make school lunches, comb the snarls out of your hysterical daughter's hair, and prod your son to get to the bus on time.

> "So this is all about the kids, without letting them
> become the center of the universe? Great."
>
> *Marcie*

_____

Your Attitude

Your attitude is the rock on which you build success. What is attitude, and how does yours affect your life?

Attitude is your worldview, your underlying strength of character, and your spiritual maturity. Attitude is what shines forth when life gets in the way of living. It is defeat or determination, it is "what's the use" or resolve, and it is immobilizing fear or persistent plodding. We all know effusive, happy types. They seem to rise above the mundane miseries life flings at them daily. They get down but pick themselves right up. I believe many of these people are genuine.

We also know dour types. They seem to be weighed down not just by life's daily blast of reality but also by the chronicle of extra troubles that have come their way. I believe many of these people are fully justified in their distrust, their anger, and their feelings of victimhood. Some people I've encountered have been positively pummeled by life. You may be one of them.

Most of us are someplace between those two types. Most of us have some days with a positive outlook, and most of us have some days that bring us to the brink of despair. If you are a single mom, some days can be "despair squared"!

Sobbed into your pillow lately? Nearly had a wreck trying to hurry from work to day care before it closes? Stayed up late in utter terror because your teen is still out? Stayed up all night with a child who will *not* stop crying? Felt the incriminating stares (at least to you they were incriminating) of others who know you had your child out of wedlock? Begun laughing like a hyena when you realized it's so long since you've shaved your legs you could braid the hair?

Of course you have.

And you think I'm going to tell you to buck up and grab life by the tail and do a do-sc-do? *No!* I'm not into trite pandering. We don't need smiley faces plastered on our refrigerators; we need to know how to stock that fridge with healthy foods our children will eat. We don't need cutesy slogans taped to bathroom mirrors; we need to look into our mirrors and see a face not ravaged by fatigue or stress or blotchy skin. We don't need some flippant author to trivialize our circumstance by heaping unrealistic ideals on us about how we *should* mother, live, or think; we need someone who understands that we are occasionally cranky and a tad ready to rip someone's ear off with our teeth.

I understand.

However, the right attitude is downright necessary for you to get through this if you want to live well. The wrong attitude will sink your ship faster than a cannonball from the SS Doomsday.

Can you have the right attitude in the midst of a dreary day? Yes—that's exactly when a right attitude manifests itself. If you are cheerful on a day of sunshine and roses, attitude has little to do with that cheer. It's all reactive emotion. If you manage to hold your head up (or screw it back on) in the midst of a day from you-know-where, *that* is where a healthy attitude reveals itself. And, Mom, you have to have a healthy attitude! Why? Because life happens, and it happens with relentless force.

You are going to wake up with gung-ho resolve, but by nine AM you'll be racing to the pantry for a bag of Ranch-flavored chips. Why? Junior flushed your cell phone down the toilet, Missy threw up when you forced her to eat oatmeal, and the washing machine spewed water on the floor. By nine AM the day was gone with the cell phone.

Of course, mothering is also filled with joy and blessing and Gerber moments. My emphasis on the hardships of single mothering is merely a nod toward those moments that aren't so endearing, that cause you to say, "This stinks! I hate what has happened to me! I feel as if I'm going to explode! I don't like facing an empty bed every night, even if it fills up with kids by morning. I'm mad as the dickens! You got a problem with that?"

No. Frankly I'm glad you're honest about how you feel. Feelings need to be heard.

Here is how a healthy attitude works: You wake up gung-ho, and life happens. Maybe you yell, maybe you kick something (not the kids or the dog)…and then you get on with life. You get on with life partly because you have no choice and partly because you have to for your well-being. Attitude is reflected in how you react. You cannot live well in *any* circumstance if you have a poopy attitude. Let your actions reflect a healthy attitude today. (For sure, other factors enter into our reactions, such as hormones, our health, and our diets.)

Someday you will face an empty nest, and then you can turn your concentration from child-rearing toward glorious independence, self-realization, and self-fulfillment. Do what you can now to ensure that you will enter that time with a body, mind, and spirit that are fit and not fitfully ravaged from stress or negative emotions that come from a persistently unhealthy attitude. Find humor in your life and giggle more. In an article on laughter, one author wrote, "A growing trend of other evidence has suggested that negative emotions, particularly depression and stress, can be harmful, making people more prone to illness, more likely to experience suffering from their ailments and less likely to recover as quickly, or at all."[1]

How do you know if you have a healthy attitude? Consult three expert sources: yourself, a close friend, and your children.

Some Questions to Ask Yourself

Put a bookmark in this page and ponder the following questions before you go to bed. Sleep on them. How is your attitude—your worldview, your strength of character, and your spiritual maturity—represented by your thoughts and your behavior?

1. When I've had arguments with others (including my ex), what accusations do they make about my personality and character? Do their statements about me carry any truth?

2. What positive things do people say about me?

3. Am I moody and pessimistic? If so, do I have a clue why?

4. Am I ever satisfied? If not, why can't I be happy with my circumstance?

5. When am I truly happy?

6. Am I angry? If so, who am I angry with and why?

7. Is my heart broken? If so, who broke it and why?

8. Do I feel inadequate...

   a. because of my childhood?

   b. because other people have told me I am inadequate?

   c. because of my incomplete education?

   d. because of my seeming inability to cope?

   e. because my children aren't as adjusted as I'd like?

   f. because my children don't seem to respect me?

9. Am I jealous of women who have the companionship of a good man with whom they share the responsibility of child rearing?

10. Am I lonely? Are unmet needs driving my behavior?

11. Am I passive? Do I accept everything that comes my way as God's will?

12. What one word describes my attitude before bearing children?

13. What one word describes my attitude after bearing children?

14. Do I concentrate on my faults or failures and therefore dwell on the negatives?

15. What positive things can I say about my behavior and personality?

Consult a Close Friend

Call a trusted friend and ask her to help you with this project. Meet with your friend someplace safe from interruption. Ask her to avoid that "brutally frank" nonsense and speak gently as she shares observations about your behavior patterns. Go to your meeting with a sense of humor. Do not take baseball bats, boxing gloves, or a litany of things you'd like to see changed in *her!* You might say something like this:

"This book I'm reading said I can't go any further until I meet with someone I value and ask that person to help me sort through my reactions to things. The idea is that once I isolate some trigger points or behavior issues, I may be able to look into the matter more deeply and find help to overcome any negative patterns in my attitude. I mean, can you imagine? Me? Negative patterns?"

Once you meet with your friend, slip this page under her nose:

1. Please describe your friend's strength of character.

2. Please describe why you admire her.

3. Please look into her eyes and affirm what her friendship means to you.

4. Please tell your friend, with kindness, what worries you when you think of her.

5. Please tell your friend what simple change she could make that would help her to cope during hard times.

6. Please tell your friend what you feel derails her.

7. Please hug your friend.

8. If you are not a single mom, please read this book to better understand your friend's circumstance.

Consult Your Children

When we are outside our comfort zone, we often put on our best behavior and successfully stuff our feelings rather than express our true emotions. But put us in our families, where we are safe, and watch out below! We unleash, often in the direction of our children.

Children are savvy about reading our emotions. They know how to push buttons and how to take control of our feelings. They know just how long to nag, when we will relent, what approach will get the best results, and how to exploit a situation. They also know when they need to get out of the way or when things are truly dire. Have an age-appropriate talk with them.

Younger Children

For the youngest children, a simple appraisal of body language might be all the feedback you need. You might ask easy questions:

1. How does your tummy feel when Mommy yells?
2. What do you want to do when Mommy cries?
3. What would you like to say when Mommy isn't happy?
4. What do you like to do best with Mommy?

Incidentally, body language is more than a barometer of our reactions. According to psychologists Paul Ekman and Silvan Tomkins, body reactions (specifically facial gestures) can *cause* reactions. These two professionals have identified about 3000 facial expressions that display our emotions. They discovered that "expression alone is sufficient to create marked changes in the autonomic nervous system." They found that when they made unhappy expressions, they felt terrible and generated sadness and anguish. Angry facial expressions generated anger.[2]

Older Children

You can approach older children over pizza (if pizza isn't a common denominator and leveler of all ages, I don't know what is) or during an aimless drive through the country. You might say something like this: "I love you. But I wonder if sometimes my love is not as steady as I'd like it to be. Are there any specific issues about me that you'd like to talk about? This is a free pass, and I certainly hope you will feel safe to share concerns. Just be fair...I am behind the wheel, you know."

Be prepared. From what I've read, older kids might have a lot more going on than making dear old Mom feel good about herself. Discipline issues could spill out, and teen girls have a penchant for drama. Try to bring the conversation back to where you started:

"This is not the time to discuss your conduct or attitude, but mine. What do you think are the strengths of my character? What do you think are my weaknesses? Have I in any way unfairly burdened you with my problems?"

You are not asking your children to rate your effectiveness as a single parent, though a slew of unexpected replies may come flying across the dashboard. Your children may likely be dealing with emotional responses themselves. Unless you are a single mom by choice or have been a single mom since your child's birth and formative years, your children may be experiencing the same anger, bewilderment, and loss that you are.

I do not suggest that all children feel this way. I'm simply reminding you that your children are coping too. (More on this later in this chapter.) This is not easy for them to live with or to resolve. Human emotions are powerful forces. If we didn't have emotions we'd be dead. And you, single mom, are very much alive.

A good attitude will make a world of difference in how you fare physically, mentally, and spiritually. I urge you to aim for a healthy attitude today—just today—and allow that healthy attitude to produce healthy human reactions and relations.

Listen to the words of Arun Gandhi:

> Keep your thoughts positive because thoughts will become your words. Keep your words positive because words will become your behavior.[3]

Your Attitude Toward Your Children

Before we visit a few choice human reactions, I want to share a grave concern of mine that extends to all parents. It's about our attitude toward our children. Specifically, it is about how we talk to our children.

I was not the smartest mother on the block, but this I knew for certain: My child needed honest edification and assurance, not fakey feel-good and not haranguing. I would cut out my tongue before I would say anything in front of my child that made him feel demeaned or unwanted, or made him believe he was the cause of my troubles or a nuisance. We naturally harangue others and lash out when we are not coping, so be extra vigilant around your children.

I have recoiled in shock when I have heard parents berate their children or say abhorrent things in front of them. Watch what you say! Consider these comments:

- "You're just like your father."
- "Your father is a worthless bum." (If he is, your kids will figure it out without your input.)
- "You're the reason I'm in this predicament."
- "Life would be easier without you."
- "I can't wait until you grow up and get out on your own."
- "I wish you were never born."
- "You are so…"
- "You drive me crazy!"

You must also be careful not to demean your children's biological father. I know this is hard. You may not be perfect in this regard, but try to not encourage ill thought. This also applies to the father's extended family.

Try your best not to sharpen your children's feelings of pain or abandonment, and recognize that more than likely your children now have all their eggs in one basket. That would be you. They trust you, they rely on you, and they get everything from you. Don't give them an earful.

One woman I talked with holds serious rancor toward her ex. She told me she bites her tongue until it bleeds. "After all," she said, "how would I like it if someone dissed *my* father?"

There is yet another reason you should watch what you say in front of your children, including your sophisticated teens. Think twice, Mom, before you whine about how hard life is, how little time you have to get things done, how stressed you are, how miserable you are at work, on and on. If children hear this depressing litany, they may ask themselves, *Why on earth would I want to grow up?*

Triggers That Inflame Reaction

What about your reactive emotions, those menacing tentacles that spring from an unhealthy attitude? What provokes them? Consider these four triggers that inflame your emotional reactions:

1. Foremost is your situation and the strain it puts upon you.

2. Next is the reason for your situation: Your child's father may have abandoned you, left you, or died.

3. After that, you may be dealing with your children's father's behavior and conduct.

4. Finally, you may be dealing with your children's reaction to the situation, or with discipline problems.

A big load for anyone's shoulders.

Some Reactive Emotions: Unforgiveness and Resentment

Unforgiveness and resentment seem to be conjoined at the hip. They are almost inseparable, feeding off each other. They certainly feed off of you: Unforgiveness will eat away your health like a big worm moving silently inside your chest until it saps all the heart you have. Put it on the Lord's plate. Pray something like this: *I know I'm supposed to forgive so and so, and I sort of (or truly) want to. But I can't seem to do it. So here it is. I want to be free so I can live well according to Your will and purpose. I don't want a big worm eating away my insides.*

I have been hurt by others. The hurt has come in both physical and nonphysical forms. I do not for a heartbeat believe any of that abuse was God's will for my life. But He is undeniably using the abuse in His plan for my life now. He is using it to reach you by giving me a voice of experience—maybe an experience like yours. He is turning bad stuff into blessing.

Ask God to turn the bad stuff you have endured—and any unforgiveness or resentment that comes from it—into blessing. If you don't, it will suffocate the life right out of you. You would be letting the person who hurt you continue to hurt you. Forgiveness is about freedom and health. It's also about obedience. True forgiveness is a copy of God's forgiveness and is made possible by it.[4]

I am not talking about retribution, and I am not talking about reconciliation. I am not even talking about forgiving someone only if he has asked for forgiveness.

I am talking about breaking free of the bondage unforgiveness holds on you. Forgiving others for your own sake. You want to live well, right? Free your heart and let go of whatever is eating you alive.

> "You spend all your energy planning how to get even?
> *There's* a healthy hobby."
>
> *Marcie*

Anger

People nowadays seem to be touchier, more sensitive, and way too quick to be offended and to get mad. We get mad for many reasons: when people insult us, when our children misbehave, when our world seems to be spiraling out of control, when we have an argument, when we are running late, when we spill gasoline on our favorite jeans (or outgrow them), when we get a parking ticket. I'm talking beyond mad; I'm talking anger. Deep stuff. Anger that stains and smells up every day like that gasoline leak on your jeans. Anger that often comes from feeling out of control or from sincere pain. Anger that is seared onto our hearts like grill marks on mahimahi.

Anger can hibernate in hidden heart nooks and suddenly wake up ready to whop the world. A lifetime of burying the emotional impact of abuse can create a significant storehouse of pain that has to escape.

Your husband or partner left you, or he died, or he never wanted you or your children in the first place. He's a bum. Life isn't always fair, but it's all you have. Harold Graham of Fellowship Missionary Church in Fort Wayne, Indiana, says it well: "Anger literally begins to rot you out on the inside." Remember the worm of unforgiveness? He has relatives.

You have two choices: Do something about the anger in your life or don't do something about it. If you're interested in doing something, here are some suggestions:

- Pray.

- Join an anger management group.

- Seek counsel from a professional or from a trusted pastor.

- If you are an angry Christian, ask yourself, *What kind of witness am I giving to a watching world?* You might also ask yourself, *What kind of witness am I giving to my children?*

- If possible, avoid environments (or people) who will push your buttons. Jesus calls us to be peacemakers and to be reconciled to each other, but you'll have time enough to be Christlike to that certain person when you are more secure. If you face an anger problem, a little space from button-pushers might make sense.

- Prepare to have a healthy response for the moments when your hot buttons are pushed. I heartily recommend taking Scripture to heart:

Do not be wise in your own eyes; fear the LORD and shun evil. This will bring health to your body and nourishment to your bones (Proverbs 3:7-8).

There are six things the LORD hates, seven that are detestable to him: haughty eyes, a lying tongue, hands that shed innocent blood, a heart that devises wicked schemes, feet that are quick to rush into evil, a false witness who pours out lies, and a man who stirs up dissension among brothers (Proverbs 6:16-19).

A gentle answer turns away wrath, but a harsh word stirs up anger (Proverbs 15:1).

Do not say, "I'll do to him as he has done to me; I'll pay that man back for what he did" (Proverbs 24:29).

Do you see a man who speaks in haste? There is more hope for a fool than for him (Proverbs 29:20).

(For good measure read James 3:1-12.)

Loss and Heartbreak

He Rejected You

How do you cope with outright rejection? I mean, doesn't the guy have a conscience? He's walked out and left you with children. And you're supposed to suck it up and have the right attitude? It's all you can do to breathe!

Carly may have just as well been flattened by a Greyhound. Jack was doting, attentive, hip—and the one to campaign for children so soon into their relationship. Two kids later he left, off to woo another woman with the same lies. Shock, fury, jealousy, and depression collided in Carly as her self-worth took a direct hit. All her begging, threatening, and cajoling would not win Jack back. News of his wedding sent Carly into a depressed state that lasted four years.

Don't let that happen to you. Alright…four months, maybe— you *are* human. If that happened to me, I'd be depressed too. But four years? Any guess what the quality of life was for Carly and her children during those years? I'll let her tell you:

> After a while I gave up on everything and didn't care. My weight skyrocketed and so did my kids' weight. There were nights I served bags of chips with dip and just gave the kids a carton of yogurt. To keep from crying myself to sleep I became addicted to a computer game. I was a mess until I joined a divorce recovery group at church and began to take control of my life. My kids really suffered.

Adding to this loss may be the loss of the father's extended family or of friends. These are times when loyalties are drawn in the sand. These are also times when awkward strain enters previously fine relationships.

He Died

People have labored lifetimes trying to understand why God would allow suffering. I believe God gets more credit than He deserves.

Yes, He allows things to happen. He allowed your husband to die—it is no solace to know that only He knows why. Our limited intellects cannot comprehend why the very God we turn to would allow such hurt. Some things we will only understand when we are face-to-face with Him, looking in the glass clearly. Coping and living our life to His glory may feel like a cruel and impossible mission. Yet His promise to us is that He is with us every inch of the way.

When a spouse dies, the feeling of abandonment is overwhelming, the sorrow too great to bear. I'm not going to tell you that "God does not give us more than we can handle." Of *course* this could seem like more than you can handle. For heaven's sake, your husband died, and you have kids! But you have no choice…because of the kids.

Guilt

Some popular pundits think guilt is totally wacko. Guilt is consigned to our "primitive, puritanical past" and has no place in the hearts and minds of postmodern people. Oh, please. Show me a single mom who has to drag her kids out of bed and leave them at day care (sick or healthy, screaming or content) who has never felt a tinge of guilt, and I'll show you a bald-faced phony or someone so indoctrinated by feel-good philosophy that she is out of touch with real emotions. Of course you feel guilty from time to time! Even if you were a stay-at-home co-parent you'd occasionally face guilt over your child rearing capabilities.

One writer put it this way, "Mothering is about never being able to give enough and feeling guilty about that."[5]

You may feel guilt because you contributed to (or initiated) the separation that cost the kids the presence of a father they adore. You may feel guilt because you have to leave them in order to go to work. You may feel guilt because you can't give them everything you'd like. (In my perspective, a very good thing.) You may feel guilt because of where you and the children are forced to live, what you feed them, where they go to school, the lack of money for summer camps and vacations. A mother in Virginia told me, "I hurt. I sacrifice my feelings for my son." You may even feel guilt because you sometimes resent having children. (News flash: Resenting them from time to time is normal. If you resent them *most* of the time, you'd better seek counsel. Fast.)

"I mean, you spend your whole life putting yourself first,
and now—*poof!*—you're second."
Marcie

What you do with your guilt becomes critical. Don't punish yourself, and don't spend all your energy trying to compensate your children. Your marriage is over. If you're harboring guilt, it still owns you. Ditto hate, by the way. According to Dr. Carl Pickhardt, "Love and loathing are both passionate connections, and the divorce reactor is still 'wed' to the ex through hate."[6]

Whatever your circumstance, whatever the reason for your circumstance, it is your circumstance. Get on with it. This is one place I will use a slogan: Don't cry over split milk. This is your life now, if only for a season. If you let guilt cripple you, you'll not be able to provide the security your children must have.

On the other hand, guilt may be a call for contrition and repentance because of sin. Contrition means saying you're sorry; repentance means turning your back on the sin you are sorry for. In Scripture we read of a merciful God who forgives and forgets iniquity, who removes our sin from us as far as the east is from the west. If you are truly guilty because of sin, try praying this prayer: *Lord, I have this guilt haunting me. It's about _____. I'm relying on Your promise to remember this no more. I need You to help me not to remember too. I've got these kids to raise, and I want to do the best I can. I can't do it without You. Help!*

Pray something like that.

Loneliness

At least mothers who aren't alone have a warm body to sleep next to every night, regardless of how isolated they feel day in and out. You may have companionship through work or through friends, but it's that bedroom at night, isn't it? Or making tough decisions on your own, like whether to fix the car or sell it, or how to address the issue of intimacy with your son, or when to trust your daughter with her own debit card. All those things are hard for you, but the aloneness, away from touch, away from that part of your femininity that is aching to be fulfilled—that is harder.

In the next chapter I will discuss the issue of dating and the importance of friends. But you are right: This is one of the hardest parts. Sherri said it well:

> You'd be surprised. Some of the most progressive people in this town just dropped me like a hot potato when Tom and I divorced. We were a power couple. Not only am I divorced from Tom, now it's like I'm divorced from my friends. It galls me that they have the nerve to invite him to their functions and ignore me. Tom! The one who had the affair!

Not fair, is it? Yet it happens all the time.

Can you be alone without feeling lonely? I believe you can. Here are some things to remember:

- This is only for a season. Motherhood never ends, but mothering does.

- Initiate relationship. Be open to new associations or put yourself in environments where some of your loneliness may be abated.

- Find an activity that is self-indulgent. Do something satisfying that enhances your sense of accomplishment and promotes self-worth. Learn how to play a musical instrument or buy a fat spiral notebook and write about your life. Turn your kitchen into a cook's haven. Go to school.

- Embrace that which leads to peace.

Inner Peace

I am certain we cannot have inner peace without the intervening work of God. Jesus said, "Peace I leave with you; my peace I give you. I do not give to you as the world gives. Do not let your hearts be troubled and do not be afraid" (John 14:27). Bonita put it this way: "I know it's not me because there were days I didn't want to live anymore, days I was contemplating suicide. I became angry, I cried. Each and every day I've got to submit to His will and His way. That's how I cope."

When your child runs to you and is hurt or fearful, what do you do to bring peace to the child's heart? You hold the child in your arms and quiet him or her. "Shhh," you say; "shhh," you coo. "It will be okay. Calm down...shhh." Put yourself in Jesus' arms for a second, feel His love, and listen—listen closely as Jesus says, *Shhh...do not be afraid.* Jesus' most repeated instruction was just that: Do not be afraid.

I have read that God cannot be contemplated or defined with mere words but can be met in silence. I encourage you to squeeze the practice of silence into a few minutes each day. Silence, or silent contemplation, is one sure path to inner peace. Odds are the world inside your house is filled with clamor and noise.

I urge you to consider establishing a "quiet time," a defined period of time when you and the children can decompress after the push and noise of a busy day. Designate 15 minutes in the evening and call it a noise-free zone. This includes not using headphones!

Fear and Worry

"My number one fear is that my children will some day look back and blame me for everything, and I feel guilty that I didn't pick a better father for them. I don't want my kids to hate me for not being able to provide what they desire as well as what they need."

Bonita

How do you tame the terror inside you so you can raise the little terror that may be running through the house right now? Through a healthy attitude, through books like this, through helpful networks, through church involvement, through proper care of yourself, and through prayer. For now, let me make one strong recommendation: Don't look at the big picture.

The big picture can scare the tar out of us. Bring it down to a manageable frame. That is why I told you I am only interested in today. Today is a hiccup when you consider the years you face in your status as a single mom. Bonita puts it this way, "I try not to think beyond today because that's all I have." I am not suggesting you abandon all cares and expect life to be a magic carpet ride. I'm not suggesting you hold no concern for the future. I am suggesting you abandon unproductive and fruitless worry over things you cannot control. Yes, you are alone and the only adult in the home. Yes, you have to cope with caring for the house, the car, and the kids. Yes, you are responsible for the bills, and you have to learn everything you can to lessen the drain on your wallet (chapter 6 is loaded with help), but you are sitting under a roof right now. It might not be much. You might even be in a shelter, but today, this minute, you're under a roof.

I suggest you write a daily prayer. Storm the very throne room of God with petition to get through today. Here's a sample:

Dear Father, You know my heart; You know my circumstance. When I look at the big picture, it's pretty scary stuff. Today is about all I can handle. I'm begging You for mercy and grace to get through today—just today. I pray this in Your Son's name. Thank You.

Depression

Anxiety and depression go hand in hand. Some depression may be healthy and might be a healing response to certain experiences. You may be depressed for a while after your loss. The morning is coming, however, when you will wake up, look in the mirror, and say, "Enough," and you'll get on with life in a more positive manner. But you may have catapulted into a black hole. You may be suffering from melancholy or despair and be utterly miserable. Perhaps you are in full-out depression.

Some of us cannot "fix" depression with a cute phrase, with determination to overcome, or with a writer's cheering and goodwill.

For some, the relentless agony of depression can lead to thoughts of suicide. If depression lasts longer than a short while, please talk to a professional. Putting yourself and your children through this does not make sense. Black holes are no fun.

Strong warning: Depression can lead to suicide. If you have suicidal thoughts, seek professional help at once.

Children Need to Cope Too

Odds are your children are facing loss through a feeling of abandonment. This loss has the potential of looming large in a child's life and becoming the child's primary focus. Profound insecurity can result. How well are your children coping?

Children interpret and respond to circumstances quite differently than adults do. Children, especially the very young, cannot deal well with abstracts. They deal in tangible and easily explainable evidence from their environment. They look to their parents for stability and security within that environment. Insecurity can manifest itself in a myriad of ways, from misbehavior to fears to sudden ritualistic behavior. A child who is coping with loss or abandonment needs massive doses of assurance that you will not also leave. Daddy never came home—how is the child to know you will?

Children of all ages need careful attention when transitioning to a mom-only household. Throw those "horrible-moans" (hormones) of adolescence into the mix and you may have your hands full. Loss can exacerbate normal teen rebellion or be channeled into depression or destructive behavior.

Strength of character does come from adversity. Give children the resources and support they need to weather this time and develop that character. Voicing their hurts and fears in a safe environment that consistently reinforces their worth and security will help them to do so.

Both you and your children may harbor an unhealthy fear of commitment as a result of your loss. Vigilantly keep communications open and perhaps consider counseling. If you are having trouble reasoning through your loss or coping emotionally or spiritually, can you imagine what a little person is facing? Many schools offer counseling groups to help kids through divorce, and most large churches provide grief consel.

Be Careful How You Verbalize Loss

Many adults are walking around with a bitterness and anger toward God because of misconceptions ladled out to them in times of trauma when they were young. You must never, ever assume you know what a child is seeing and thinking. If you are dealing with children and loss, you must consistently communicate with the child at the child's level with as much honesty as possible. Remain honest with a child without being brutally graphic when presenting facts. Be careful not to advance your fears about loss to a child, especially if someone has died.

In a book called *How to Tell the Children*, Dan Schaefer and Christine Lyons give this caution: "Avoiding the issue or making up fairy tales to explain away death are devices that almost always fall apart."[7]

If the father has died, do not tell children that he "went to sleep" one day and did not awaken. Children can become mighty fearful of sleep as a result of that notion.

Do not say that Dad has just "gone away" or has been lost. A young mind will reason that Daddy abandoned him or her on purpose or will come home someday. And if he's lost, can't we just find him?

Rather than telling children that it is God's will that Daddy is gone or that God "takes people," say that when people die and are dead they will be with God.

Make it your business to know what other people are telling your child, adults as well as children. This is important because misguided adults can scare the wits out of young children who cannot grasp philosophical or spiritual terms. Adults can be incredibly insensitive to the feelings of children. We often say things to children that we would never utter to another adult. Your children are mourning, whether through divorce or death. Everyone's sorrow is unique.

Older Children

Most teenagers are up to their eyeballs in schoolwork, peer pressure, and hormonal activity that has them singing for joy one day and singing the blues the next. They are right on the line between being fully grown and being a child. Emotions and longings tug at them from both directions. It is a very hard time.

Dealing with loss compounds and complicates a teen's life further. It may bring a teen to the brink of not being able to cope. When we cannot cope, we develop methods or ploys or personalities that help us to cope. Some of these are healthy, some are not. Be especially aware of the needs of your teens as they face significant loss. A teenager could feel a good amount of self-pity, frustration, and fear if suddenly thrust into this situation.

Parental Inversion

Expecting moral support and assistance from an older child is not unreasonable. Just watch out for the possibility of parental inversion. Parental inversion happens when a child takes the responsibility to become a peer—or parent—to the remaining parent. This is not a cool thing. It happened to me.

Recognizing my father's failure, I became one whale of a worker and achiever. At some eerie levels, I became a "husband" to my mother, helping with child care, laundry, home repair, and emotional support. Sometimes she expected this of me, and sometimes I voluntarily stepped into the void. A book by John and Paula Sandford enlightened me: My hard work was not so much to earn love as to keep the world of fear and chaos from me. Their words still ring a bell:

> When one parent fails or is gone from home, one of the children, usually the eldest of the opposite sex, steps in to fill the vacant spot. A son may become the breadwinner. He may become the mother's confidant or her strength to lean upon. He may disciple the younger children. In short, in one degree or another, he may set about to run the household in his father's place. That puts him in position of a husband—without the bed.[8]

Be careful not to overburden your older children or to rob them of their childhoods. Stepping in and helping out is important and should be encouraged, but maintaining structure, stability, and control for your children is up to you.

A Good Choice: Hope

Hope is an emotional sort of thing, knotted tightly into our feelings, leaving great black holes when it dies. Hope is necessary for you. Those who cling to the belief that God keeps His promises have inner confidence and hope. This brings a serenity that the world cannot match. You can nurture hope through constancy and through fixed goals.

Being Constant

Being "up" all the time is impossible. You may feel you have to stay "up" for the children, to not let your guard down, to be nothing but perfect, and to be able to remedy any problem that may come your way. That is not the constancy I am talking about.

What I mean when I talk about being constant is the slow, plodding, step-step-step that comes from the determination to succeed at this thing called motherhood.

Fixing Goals

Here again I may fool you. The goal setting I am talking about is not heroic, like getting your PhD while raising perfect children in a country setting complete with an organic garden and perfectly trimmed rose bushes. When I talk about goals, I mean a daily routine that ties into constancy quite nicely. Earlier I suggested establishing a "quiet time" for the entire family. Suppose you agree that from 7:00 to 7:15 PM the house will be silent—and suppose you actually got into the practice of maintaining that silence routinely. That is a goal. It is definable and attainable.

Routines can include eating dinner as a family every night, going to the bakery every Saturday morning, having soup every Monday night, or visiting Gram and Gramps every other Sunday afternoon.

Such goals will not only add a spark of anticipation and pleasure but will also distract from everyday struggles.

> "A lot of women think they're starting over.
> Me? I'm just continuing."
> *Marcie*

Strengths of the Single Mom

Once you get the hang of it, being a single mom means coping quite well. This is a good place to share the positive traits of being a single mom. Dr. Carl Pickhardt mentions many strengths of the single parent. Single parents...

1. are highly committed

2. are clear communicators

3. are firm decision makers

4. are well organized

5. manage diverse family functions

6. create a network of social support

7. have clear priorities
8. value family values
9. are good at making ends meet
10. give children clear expectations
11. give children family responsibilities
12. are realistic about setting limits[9]

──────────── RESOURCES ────────────

Dr. Carl Pickhardt has written several helpful books and offers infomative online articles about parenting. (www.carlpickhardt.com)

Parents Anonymous, the nation's oldest child abuse prevention organization, is dedicated to strengthening families and building caring communities that support safe and nurturing homes for all children. (909-621-6184, www.parentsanonymous.org)

──────────── READING ────────────

Carl Pickhardt, *The Everything Parent's Guide to Positive Discipline* (Avon, MA: Adams Media, 2003).

Ken Sande, *The Peacemaker: A Biblical Guide to Resolving Personal Conflict* (Grand Rapids, MI: Baker Book House, 1991).

Tim LaHaye and Bob Phillips, *Anger Is a Choice* (Grand Rapids, MI: Zondervan, 2002).

Kathy Koch, *Finding Authentic Hope and Wholeness* (Chicago: Moody Press, 2005).

Pat Holt and Grace Ketterman, *When You Feel Like Screaming* (Colorado Springs: WaterBrook Press, 2001).

Three

Leaning on Others

It's a snow day and the kids are home. You must go to work. Day care is closed. Their father is out of the picture. Whom do you call?

Your car is constantly breaking down. You need honest advice whether to keep it or trade it in. Whom do you call?

You cannot get through another day. Dark thoughts enter your mind. You feel utterly despondent. Whom do you call?

Never Walk Alone

You may be the only active parent, but trying to tackle this job alone would be ridiculous. Don't buy into the notion that to be a strong woman you should not ask for help. Regardless of how isolated or burdened you feel, help is available. You're holding help in your hands right now. A book can empower you to live well and to parent well. Yet books are not the same as a living, breathing person with arms to hold, hands to help, and ears to hear.

Many single moms do not have friends—or have lost the friends they once had. Why do single moms often find themselves bereft of close, abiding friendships? Listen to one single mom from Texas: "I have family that helps when they can, but friendships are harder to maintain...I guess I don't really have anyone I feel that close to."

And a single mom from Virginia: "I know I should find me some friends, but I just don't trust nobody. I know that's bad, but I've been hurt."

And then there is Marcie: "Friends?! You gotta be kidding! Maybe conversation with the other moms in play group. My friends from before treat me like I'm a pariah, like I'm going to steal their husbands. Who needs them?"

You do. Healing and coping can come from knowing you are not alone. Just knowing you have someone or something to fall back on—a safety net—may give you the strength to persevere.

Isolation

Isolation is terrific for the religious ascetic living in a cave in the Gobi Desert; it is not good for anyone else. Isolation is not healthy for body, mind, or spirit. Isolation hurts. If you doubt this, think of the effect isolation has in punishment, from sending a child into another room for time-out to solitary confinement in prison. Humans need interaction with one another as a matter of survival. Take Shane, for instance, who is the mother of three young children. Talking with other mothers in similar situations helps her to cope. Yet there you are, a single mom most likely isolated from those you need in order to survive. What happened?

Loss of Solidarity

For one thing, female bonding has been eroding since the turbulent

1960s, and an unspoken code of sisterhood, support, and friendship has suffered. Rest easy—I am not one to wax nostalgic about some fanciful version of the past. We women have come a long way, and much of that is good.

But efforts to empower and equalize women may have been one of those "baby-bathwater" things, generating full-blown phobia toward traditional family models and outright fear of any impediment to individual autonomy. For the most part, we simply are not there for each other anymore. This cultural lessening of female bonding contributes to a feeling of isolation.

Children

Children have a tendency to distance us from routine social encounter. Many mothers (of young children, in particular) feel the loss of social capital—the rich fabric of friends and acquaintances who share enough in common to contribute to each other's well-being. Social capital also includes association through shared environment—the heady rush you feel in a crowded bookstore, the stimulation of a bustling farmer's market, the chance to sit in a stadium and enjoy a sports event. Mothers often feel as if they've been kidnapped and transported to a different planet where juice cups and colorful plastic and noisy toys abound. They are wrenched from life as they knew it to life as it is now: children and their needs. Freedom either evaporates or is limited to rare moments that usually require advance planning and tiring preparations. Spontaneity is gone; you can't walk out the door and drive to the coffeehouse at whim. Such freedom is seriously impeded by diaper bags and car seats and school schedules and food fights and bedtime stories. You're cool with that—you like being a mother, even though it does seem to be isolating at times. Add the twist of being a single mom, though, and watch that isolation escalate.

Compartmentalization

Regardless of how convincing the magazine articles are, and regardless of the propaganda on talk TV about the glories of singleness and the evils of traditional marriage, I've observed an undeniable instinct to couple up. I am intrigued that the same magazines that promote self over conventional coupling invariably include articles on how to become more attractive, how to get your man, dating, and marriage. What does this have to do with the isolation of the single mom? This: We live in a couples-dominant society. Aside from church, family events, and weddings, how common are social functions with a mix of couples, single men, and single women? I sense if we looked closely we would find such functions more the exception than the rule. To socialize as singles, many people herd into singles categories. Though this is understandable, it brings home my point: We tend to compartmentalize—couples here, singles here, oldsters here, youngsters here. Some of this is normal and natural. But couples-dominant society and the compartmentalization it enforces is harmful to community as we separate not only generationally but also by marital status and gender. We are disconnected from one another and distinguished within that disconnect. So among others, we have couples (with kids) and singles (without kids). Where is the single mom in this group distinction? Often at the bottom of the food chain.

Social Discomfort

Related to the couples-only mind-set or the single-and-free mind-set is the nagging question of why the single mom (and the divorced mom, in particular) is suddenly disenfranchised from social constructs. Though friends may offer an initial show of support, what happens over time? Many women relate that they find themselves the odd woman out. As Sherri said in the last chapter, she found herself off guest lists which, to her sheer amazement, continued to include her adulterous husband.

The adage "time heals all wounds" does not always ring true. It is common for the ex-wife of a total cad to spend weekend nights in front of her TV with a bowl of popcorn while he glad-hands old friends. Never mind any thoughts of romance for these women (nice as it would be to know they could still attract a man). How pleasant would it be just to be included as a valued guest at someone's home?

Protocol

Without a protocol, people often back off because they are uncertain of what to do or say. No code of behavior is in place for relating to folks who are divorced, which is a bit odd considering 50 percent or so of us go through divorce. Sure, an ex-spouse will receive the initial concerned phone calls and pledges of allegiance, but time dulls zeal. A sense of relief follows quickly when the now-single woman rejects an invitation, vindicating us permanently from issuing invitations again. Seldom do people recognize that divorcees and widows need time to heal or to feel confident about accepting invitations.

Some protocol is in place for when someone's spouse dies: condolence calls, cards, and offers to help. But what do we do six months later? A year later? I'll tell you what many of us do: We see the woman at the market and make a fast U-turn with our cart, we avoid real eye contact at church, we get all flustered when we address Christmas cards. Little or no protocol exists for what to do or say beyond the graveyard.

Too Busy

A huge reason for isolation is busyness. Most parents—and single moms in particular—do not have the time or the energy to cultivate and nurture relationships. They could not fit one more thing into their lives if they had a shoehorn and axle grease. To have to sustain a relationship or feel encumbered with responsibility to reciprocate someone's attention is too much. As I wrote in *Ditch the Diet and the*

Budget, when we are busy, friendship is the first thing to go. Many of us are booked solid, and our busyness causes the deadly consequence of isolation. When we are exhausted or consumed, all relationships suffer.

Self-Sabotage

Will you feel awkward around old friends and couples? Maybe. To be sure, being surrounded by others like you is more comfortable. That's why we compartmentalize and why we join clubs in the first place: We like to be surrounded by others who know what we are experiencing and what we are feeling, and who can relate.

Some single moms do not feel ready to join the world but need time and space to adjust. Transition takes time. Yet while you must guard your privacy, you must also guard against creating the very isolation you may come to dread. I've spoken to women who deliberately avoid relationships due to lack of trust. Regardless of your inclination to distrust and regardless of your past disappointments and failed friendships, you need to cultivate meaningful relationships. You may rely on your friends more than they rely on you, and that's okay; friends do not care. Real friendship is not based on tit for tat.

Some of us sabotage the very relationships we need because of our personality. We may be so needy we become clinging vines, and our desperation drives people away. Some of us go into our shell and clam up when times are tough. We have learned to trust the comfort of our own counsel, and by the way, we believe we can't get hurt inside that shell. But we can—this is isolation at its worst. To make yourself vulnerable and to seek the counsel and comfort of others can be intimidating, but you must. Two hands (or more) are always better than one.

"I am mom and dad 24/7. All decisions are personal
because if it goes wrong you only have yourself to blame.
When you are sick or just completely exhausted, no one

takes over for a while. Decisions on discipline, finances, vacations, schools, doctors, even whether or not to get a family pet…all rests on your shoulders."

Shane

All Hands on Deck

"This takes a village…I am blessed with family and friends I trust."

Sheila

Relationships are made of much more than social enterprise or casual conversation. I am unflinching in my conviction that you must establish a safe, helpful network of people to help you perform your role as a single mom. You need a team, a working safety net. Before we get into creating that team, let's identify some of your actual needs.

Legal Help

You need legal help. What are the legal rights of a single mom, including rights as an employee?

In a divorce, you have more to consider than the divorce decree: child support, child visitation, alimony, health insurance, and taxes to name a few. The burden to deal justly is great in a divorce. Communication, which is usually strained and difficult, is most important. A divorce lawyer should guide you through the emotional train wreck of divorce, guard your interest, and meet all legal requirements. Lawyers usually come with a hefty price tag, so if all legal matters are satisfied and legal support is needed merely to mediate between two warring people from a failed marriage, stubbornness and anger may cost you both plenty. In some instances a Guardian ad Litem is appointed by the court. This is someone who advocates for the child during a divorce. This person is commonly an attorney.

(Keep accurate notes of conversations or agreements you have with your ex about your children. Date your entries and be honest when recording facts.)

In the case of death, you are faced with legal issues. Look for seasoned, knowledgeable professionals who deal with estates and probate. Widows have always been vulnerable in society. In Exodus 22:23-24 God promises speedy revenge upon anyone who afflicts a widow.[1]

On top of all else, don't forget to write your will. Write a will, Mom! You should be the one to declare who will be rightful guardians of your children should you die, not the courts!

Legal counsel is utterly necessary. Interview attorneys no differently than you would any other job applicant. Consult with more than one attorney so you can determine who will work best for you.

Medical Help

You need medical help and well-child help. This could range from assessing great-grandmother's healing remedies to visiting well-baby clinics, from trusted alternative care providers to your child's pediatrician, from regular dental care to your ob-gyn. I am convinced that much traditional wisdom has been lost in favor of quick-fix drug therapy. Some drugs do provide merciful relief to suffering, but much can be said for time-honored methods that mothers have relied on since time began. In addition to conventional medical practitioners, I urge you to include someone with this wisdom on your team.

Financial Help

You may need financial counseling. Rare is the single mom who does not need help financially. I urge you to consider the money-saving advice of this book, in concert with two of my previous books: Living Well on One Income and Ditch the Diet and the Budget. Taken together, these three books will give you countless strategies and practical advice to beat the money monster into submission.

Many excellent books offer guidance for everything from investing in the market to saving on the grocery bill. Though books are important, you also need a second party to whom you are accountable, someone who is trained or practiced in money management and who can guide and encourage you. This is especially important when you file your tax return each year. A knowledgeable tax advisor will often save you money.

Child Care Providers

You need regular and backup child care providers. Every parent, single or not, needs emergency child care sometime. Whom do you call in the event of bad weather, school vacation, an ill child, or your own illness? Regular child care providers can get sick or go on holiday, schools close for spring break, snow happens, flu happens, summer vacation happens. Establishing a safe and dependable backup for child care brings invaluable peace of mind. Enlisting the experience of other mothers and grandmothers for advice in child care also makes sense. (Chapter 8 is specifically dedicated to the issue of child care.)

A Life Coach

You may need help to live on your own. You have a house to take care of and a car and a yard...how *do* set the timer on the sprinkler system, anyway? And you need new administrative skills to run your family. A life coach would be nice, but who can afford one? (Again, I refer you to my books and others like them.) Who can you tap for help to order your home and your day? Do you have a friend who can help you organize your kitchen and your bedroom closets? Do you know a trustworthy mechanic who will help you keep your car on its wheels? Merchants and service providers can add immeasurable assistance toward home and car care.

You may also feel nervous or frightened to be the only adult in the home. Who can you call for moral support? Who makes you feel safe? Who can teach you how to be safe? (See chapter 11.)

Emotional Support

You need emotional support. Most single moms have as many ups and downs as the New York Stock Exchange—certainly enough to make them candidates for Bipolar Mother of the Month. You need someone on your team who will listen when you need to vent or when you are feeling low. You also need someone to fulfill your need for love and for touch—you need someone to hold you. I'm not talking about the hug thing. We hug each other all the time—when we greet each other on the street, when we pass the peace in church, when we come together for holiday celebrations. (I recently heard that we each need 12 hugs a day to maintain emotional balance.) But you need to be *held*.

If someone in your circle of family and friends (especially an older person) can fill this role, ask that person to be on your team. Tell him or her that every now and then you just want to crawl into a safe embrace and stay there for a while.

Adult Companionship

You need the company of adults. Cultivate social relationships that will engage your mind as an adult woman, and find an environment where you can enjoy yourself in the company of peers. (Showing up with dried baby snot on your shoulder is okay.) For some, work may provide all the adult interaction you need. One mom from Maryland thinks of work as her sanctuary: "I don't know what I would do without work," she says. "It's the nights that are hard."

One aspect of the need for adult relationship is the man thing. Hopefully, *the* man. Adult relationships definitely extend into dating, which we will address toward the end of this chapter.

A growing trend among single moms is to share housing. When it works well, women can address many critical issues from restricted finances to childcare. One website, www.co.abode.org, matches single mothers seeking housemates. According to the website's founder, Carmel Sullivan, "This need is especially acute among single mothers seeking affordable housing, better schools, and safe neighborhoods."[2]

Write the specific help you feel you need in each category below. Identify your needs before you assemble your dream team:

Legal needs _____

Medical needs _____

Financial needs _____

Child care needs _____

Life coach needs _____

Emotional support needs _____

Adult companionship needs _____

Other _____

Where to Turn

So where do you find this dream team? You can draw from a wealth of sources. You may have an accountant in the family, a brother who tinkers with motors, a neighbor who has nothing but free time and loneliness of her own. The quickest way to find team members is to ask, ask, ask. What lawyer did your friend use? Where do other single moms send their children to day care? Has anyone encountered an inexpensive handyman? You have many options:

Jesus Christ. Friend to the friendless, Healer of the sick and the hurt, Savior. The number one pick for your team is Jesus. Reliance on Him is a slam-dunk; He won't refuse your request. Besides, He's on your team already.

Yourself. You are the captain of this team—you are the reason for this team! You are the one who has to approach designated team members with the proposition that they participate in your life at some level. You need to do the organizing, and you are the glue that holds it all together.

Your children. Some single mothers have children who have already left the nest, some have children who are in their teens, and some have children who are preadolescents. All should be team members. (A word of caution: Watch how much burden you put on your children, watch how much you expect from them, and be wary of the parental inversion we talked about in chapter 2.) Older children can help significantly around the house, and you should expect them to lend a hand. In spite of school and extracurricular demands on the children's time, I believe all children everywhere should share the load of home care. Some older children may play an invaluable role with younger siblings during after-school hours. Consider your family a mini team within your larger team. Have meetings, make plans, review progress and individual performance…all of this over pizza, of course.

The father or the father's family. Some single mothers are fortunate to have the involvement of the children's father. There are many good men who continue to take their parental responsibilities seriously even though they have left the marriage. When the father lives nearby and is active in his children's lives, much of the parenting pressure is shared. Sadly, divorce is not always amicable. Single mothers complain bitterly that fathers undermine discipline as well as moral, spiritual, and nutritional standards the moms have established. This is rough on everyone and damaging for the children.

> "He comes waltzing in like Peter Pan. The kids run
> rampant when they are with him. They eat nothing but
> junk. He's a big hero, and I get to be the meanie who has
> to whip them back into shape when they come home."
>
> *Marcie*

Your ex-husband's new wife or close friend may play a role in the care of your children. This could be hard. True, many women are able to overcome a negative emotional response toward the new woman, others accept the other woman's presence as something they cannot control, and some women declare war. Stop. Don't let your feelings of rejection or anger cloud your judgment and behavior.

You want your children to get as much love as possible. If the relatives of their father shower them with love and dedication, they boost your children's self-worth and feelings of security. Knowing that they are an integral part of the father's family is usually healthy for kids. The trauma of loss of a dad through divorce or death is hard; to also lose grandparents and aunts and uncles and cousins might only magnify that loss. The father's extended family could be an excellent source for you to consider when putting together your team.

Your family. Where would many of us be without parents and grandparents? According to the U.S. Census Bureau, the most common multigenerational family is grandparents sharing their home with a child and grandchild. This sector recently grew more than twice as sharply as the population overall.[3] Noteworthy is the conclusion of two University of Chicago researchers who found that teenagers brought up by a single mother and at least one grandparent were more likely to go to college and less likely to smoke or drink than those who live only with their mothers.[4] Single mothers commonly live with parents or siblings until they can get on their feet. This is both trying and rewarding, demanding sacrifice from all and an agreement to check egos at the door.

In spite of the media buzz about the normative standards of family as we struggle to understand changing times, make no mistake: grandparents, parents, siblings, and other relatives all matter. As families we come together, and when we do we laugh and cry at shared memories, we identify with one another, and we are there for each other. Children, especially children of loss, need the extra boost that blood relatives can give. They need to know someone is there for them.

Friends. Make a list of your friends. Put a star next to the names of those people who are unshakable in their friendship. (You may not have names on this list yet.) Which of these friends can you ask to be on your team? What are their specific skills? Friends are particularly gifted at lending an ear.

Social agencies. From medical clinics to housing aid to legal aid to sources for food, aid agencies abound. When asking for help, do not take any rejection as the final answer, be extra vigilant when receiving money from other sources, and know how any money will affect any benefits you may receive.

Volunteers. Research organizations such as Big Brothers Big Sisters, the YMCA, and co-ops for mothers with children. Consider play groups (begin one if you have to) sharing babysitting. Look for food co-ops and clothing co-ops. If you do a little detective work (usually no more than talking to other single moms in your town), you are sure to find some nonprofit agency or organization that would happily help.

Merchants or service people. I have long promoted the principle of ownership. By ownership I mean giving other people a stake in your purchase or need for service. Get others to invest thought and help find a solution. Don't be afraid to say to a mechanic, "Look, I'm a single mom on a tight budget. I need someone to service my car as inexpensively as possible without sacrificing my family's safety. Can you help me do that?"

School. According to a survey by the Department of Education, 13 percent of the nation's 16.5 million students enrolled in higher education were single parents.[5] High schools in some areas may offer day care for young children as well as parenting classes to help young mothers transition to their new role.

Low-cost housing and day care facilities exist on college campuses across the country. Some colleges offer Women and Children programs, and scholarship opportunities are expanding.

Work. I have heard of single mothers bringing their children to work, often when the children were too young for day care or preschool. Some work environments are conducive to this; some are poor environments for children. Your place of employment may be a source for your team. Does your employer provide child care or sick days for parents when children are sick? Does it allow job sharing or irregular hours so you can arrange your workday to correspond with school hours? Do your supervisors understand the need for children to call you (within reason) while you are working?

Church. This is one of my passions. I am unwavering in my conviction that no mother (or father) should be left to fend alone in the body of Christ. I examine this further in the next chapter.

Children's Needs

Your children are the love of your life. Look at them. They seem pretty normal and adjusted, considering what you've all been through. And they certainly are worth every bit of hard work and struggle on your part. But are they all right? What kinds of needs do they have, apart from normal age-related developmental adjustment?

Some children may need counseling. Unless you have been a single mom from the birth of your children or since they were very young, children may need help coping with transition and loss, which can cause profound emotional complications. Having a third-party advocate may be invaluable for a child dealing with stress or trauma.

Children need friends and peers. Whether three years old and bonking each other over the head with plastic bats, or twelve years old and batting their heads against the wall because of hormones, kids need friends. I'm talking about pals—a tad beyond play group or the usual school-related relationship. Peers—especially central in the life of the teen—become family-like arbiters in the child's life. A wise choice of friends is one of the most significant factors in the healthy development of your children.

Children need space away from siblings and space to transition. I feel strongly that children, like adults, need a little time and space apart from each other. Individual time with Mom or age-specific play groups can provide some necessary separation. School-age children have this built in. If your children are not in school, occasional time alone, when a child can develop independent of siblings, may be a healthy practice.

Children may also need a bit of space as they transition from one parent's house to the other, yet they are often hit with a general inquisition as soon as they return from a visit to the father's home. I know you're dying to find out about their father's lifestyle, his new wife, what he said about you. But those questions only satisfy your hunger to know. When a child returns, say hello and let it go. Don't make the children take sides or feel like spies.

Children Need a Male Role Model

This may be the most pressing need in your children's life, especially if their father has been lacking. Children need a father. Yours may not have one. You work double duty to be mother and father to the children. No matter how you try, you are still the mother.

Sheila, a successful businesswoman, lists this issue as her greatest fear. "I fear my children not trusting men. I fear choosing a 'wrong' man again. I fear not providing good role models."

Andy, a mom with two robust little boys, felt fortunate that a trusted male friend would visit the home and wrestle with the boys each week her husband was deployed. She admitted her concern that the absence of her husband for extended periods might have an effect on her children. In my case, my new husband Joe added so much to my son's life that I could not. Sure, I could wield an ax, a circular saw, and a hammer; I could throw a football and teach him how to ride a horse or drive a car; I could discuss the weightier matters of the world, of abstinence, of the dangers inherent in his environment. I could wrestle with him, hug him, love him, discipline him, sing to him, teach him, cook for him, and hold his hand in the night. But I could not be a dad.

I have militantly enforced a sense of gender equality. Women are not only capable, we are more capable than men to meet certain challenges and to succeed. To say that we are equal in emotive, intuitive, and perspective activity, however, is just plain goofy. The equality I uphold is "equal though different." To deny this is nothing but nonsensical fist waving. Get over it. Men and women are different. They both bring something to the table, and in the case of child development they both play necessary roles.

This is the difference that Joe brought into my son's life. Joe provided the model, the skill set, for Josh to learn from, emulate, and incorporate or blend into what I had already provided. Josh learned a male code, a certain integrity, an understanding of life that could only come from Joe.

The critical importance of a safe and healthy male role model for girls cannot be overstated. In my case, my sisters and I still suffer the consequence of poor modeling by our father. Each of us has manifested this loss in different ways, but overall we have a deep sense of distrust, defensive maneuvering (some of that fist waving), or the inability to be vulnerable. A co-parent father who is lovingly engaged in his marriage, home, and daughters' lives will teach his daughters how to negotiate the sometimes delicate male-female relationship and, through his steady love, help them to grow into confident and secure women who will be less prone to enter into unproductive or harmful unions. In my opinion, this is something only a father can do. I can only wonder if one significant factor in our escalating divorce rate has to do with young women who are clueless about healthy male-female relationship.

A single mom friend of mine wailed, "What galls me is that when my girls were young, no one ever invited us into their homes for dinner. I wanted so badly for them to get a positive spin on a dad, wanted them to see a mother-father family in action, and wanted them to have a positive model compared to what they had seen from their own father." Of note is that the woman was deeply involved in her church.

What might your children's dream team or special places look like?

Counselors _____

Friends _____

Private space _____

Male role model _____

The Forgotten Father

Stepping aside to allow your children to have a relationship with their father, even if infrequently, can be one of the hardest aspects of single parenting.

Let me be clear: The whole purpose of this book is to advocate for single mothers. Don't let negative comments in this book toward delinquent dads or abusive men affect your overall opinion. This is a book about single moms, for single moms. The last thing I want to do is to marginalize earnest and caring fathers or to demonize wonderful dads because marriages have failed. Many fathers remain interested and involved in their children's lives.

We must never forget that many men of divorce are suffering and struggling emotionally. Men confront the same assortment of emotions we saw in chapter 2, and regrets may be plenty—not to mention feeling they have been unfairly burdened with costly child support, in spite of their devotion to their children. Millions of men are outstanding husbands and fathers. We must be careful not to denigrate men as we acknowledge the failings of some. I fully agree with the comments of Joe Kelly, executive director of the national advocacy group Dads and Daughters: "To operate from the assumption that dad is a dolt is harmful to fathers, harmful to children, and harmful to mothers."[6]

While researching for this book, I attended a parenting workshop held primarily for fathers under court order. The four-hour class was an eye-opener. Primarily attended by men from lower socioeconomic neighborhoods, I saw and felt frustration, determination, fatherly concern, and rage. Some men felt marginalized by the children's caregiver (mother) and by the system. They were ordered to pay support, to attend classes from transparenting skills to anger management, and, as one man put it, "To settle for a photo." My heart broke for those men, and I saw the mess we get in when we reject the wise counsel of Scripture. Restricting sexual intimacy to the security of marriage would have greatly lessened attendance in that class that night.

Engaging civilly with your ex-husband may be a tall order, especially if one reason you divorced was inability to communicate. Figure it out instead of duking it out. Children must come before rancor or revenge. If you are using your children as pawns for revenge, what on earth is wrong with you, woman?

I urge you to meet with the father to discuss the children on a regular basis. It may be up to you to set boundaries. Compare notes: Do the children pit you against each other? Do they say, "Dad lets me do…" or "Mom says it's all right…"?

Though he may not deserve a prominent place on the living room wall, I encourage you to have a picture of the children's dad someplace in the house. Consider hanging the father's photo in your child's room.

Dating

Most women I spoke to have deferred dating for some nebulous future time. Between loyalty toward a deceased husband or wounds not yet healed from divorce or abandonment, these women are not emotionally ready to add Mr. Might Be Right to their lives, lonely for a mate though they may be. Others feel too overwhelmed with life's demands to even think about romance. Some women feel they are poor candidates for the dating pool, not having tended to their "girly" side for some time.

One mother in Texas weighed in on this topic with some experience:

> I have dated in the past. It is really hard to find the time, and the expense of babysitting can be daunting. I won't let the kids meet someone unless it feels like the relationship is going somewhere. The last person I dated did not meet the kids until we had been together for a year. We dated for two years, and then he decided he didn't think he would ever be able to make a lifelong commitment. That is hard because not only do I have to deal with the loss but so do the kids. They have already been abandoned once...It is not fair to them to bring other people in who end up disappearing. I don't see myself dating again anytime soon—not because I don't want to but for the kids' sake.

To be sure, some women date regularly, often within the comfort of established groups. My advice? Live life, be open, and let it go. You will know when you are ready. Whether your children are ready is another matter. You have to be the judge of that.

Many single mothers are extremely sensitive and vigilant about introducing their romantic interests to their children. If you invite your dates into your home regularly or invite them to spend the night, I implore you to seriously reconsider this as a parent and as a Christian.

Sexual activity has come out from under the covers. It is treated as normal and presumed behavior. If you date anyone who expects sexual favors in return for his companionship or pressures you for "fulfillment" as a "consenting adult," ditch the guy. If he can't control his sexual urge, send him back to high school. You want a man who considers you worth waiting for and loves you enough to respect your body. You also want a man who is God-fearing and already knows all of this.

Dating the Single Dad

The odds are that you'll date a man who has children. Chances are he has partial or full custody. This arrangement adds extra layers to the experience of becoming acquainted. It may also add complications in the form of personalities. You are blending several personalities; before, all you had to deal with was each other. Still, you might find comfort in commiserating with each other over the difficulties of parenting as well as enforcing each other's parenting style.

> "I will see right through an imposter next time!"
> *Marcie*

Strong Warning

I caution you not to "balance your brokenness." Let's say you are divorced from an abusive alcoholic. Good for you. Glad you're out of that situation. Don't, however, resort to yet another abusive alcoholic just because it is what you are subconsciously accustomed to. Also, do not let your loneliness be a target for wackos, weirdos, stalkers, and hucksters on the Internet or otherwise.

If you become so desperate that you fall for some stranger over the Internet or jump too quickly into relationships with questionable characters, I urge you to reconsider your actions. For whatever reason you have already loved and lost. (You didn't make that baby by yourself.) Don't set yourself up for more loss—or worse.

Finding Physical Intimacy

I talked about the need to be held in chapter 2, as well as the need for touch. Whether you are widowed or divorced, a part of you may have shriveled and blown away from lack of attention. Or you may desperately long for the intimacy you shared with your husband. What to do?

Though I understand this emptiness in your life, the only counsel

I can give is this: As a woman alone, you are consigned to a life of chaste celibacy until such time as you marry again. Our liberated sensibilities may have changed over the years, but Scripture has not.

I want to write books that help people. I want to wave a magic wand and make things right for people. I don't want to anger people in the process. So call me a messenger and listen to this message: The Bible is replete with instruction to not have sexual relations apart from marriage. I've heard it all—the urge, the need for release, the raging hormones, the deep emotional need, the fun. Excuse me, but you are not an animal who has no control over sexual impulse. You are a special creation, created in the image of God. If you are a Christian you are a temple of God the Holy Spirit, an image bearer of Christ.

Not to mention—you have kids, for crying out loud. A letter writer to a newspaper opinion column insisted it was none of her children's business whom she brought home for the night. I share part of the columnists' response: "As long as you bring your sex life home to your kids, it is very much their business." She goes on to say, "I'm of the firm opinion that single parents should never bring assorted people home to spend the night while the children are there."[7]

What About Self-Stimulation?

What does the Bible say about self-stimulation? Nothing direct or specific. It is not singled out in Paul's list of vices in Romans 1:26-32.

A short article on self-stimulation in the *Encyclopedia of Biblical and Christian Ethics* exhorts the believer to hold the mystery of faith in pure conscience and to avoid anything that would lead to impurity of thought, word, or deed.[8] Self-stimulation provides pitfalls in this regard, and believers are urged to be sure their love is of fervent purity in Christ's service.

RESOURCES

The Sisterhood of Black Single Mothers provides education and support to help black single mothers and their families, including youth awareness projects. (718-638-0413)

The National Black Child Development Institute's mission is to improve and protect the lives of children, to improve child welfare services, to make universal early care and education a reality, to build family support services, to press for educational reform, and to provide vital information on children's health. (202-833-2220, www.nbcdi.org)

Parents Without Partners provides single parents and their children with an opportunity for enhancing personal growth, self-confidence, and sensitivity toward others by offering an environment for support, friendship, and the exchange of parenting techniques. (561-391-8833, www.parentswithoutpartners.org)

Big Brothers Big Sisters of America claims to be the oldest, largest, and most effective youth mentoring association in America. Some local groups have specific outreach to children of prisoners. (215-567-7000, www.bbbsa.org)

Raising Our Kids offers advice and friendship to guide and support you through the trials and tribulations of raising children. Their site offers a large variety of resources including parenting articles, advice, free coloring pages, links to useful websites, message boards, and just about anything else a parent or grandparent could want. (www.raisingourkids.com)

Children's Rights Council, formed in 1985, is dedicated to continuing a child's contact with both parents. (301-559-3120, www.gocrc.com)

Four

Leaning on the Lord

"My state of affairs draws me closer to God, much closer.
When I felt alone and didn't have friends,
God was all I had. I've been in what I call my 'waiting
room' with Him for a long time now."

Bonita

A Short Testimony

As a single mom I worked hard to hold together a rapidly disintegrating world. Besides a day job, I began each workday cleaning hotel rooms and ended each day sweeping a produce warehouse in exchange for fruit and vegetables. My son was left to his own devices much of this time—a very tall order for a seven-year-old.

In room 43 of the resort where I cleaned bathrooms and changed sheets, I would kneel beside the bed and pray. I can now look back and see that God heard my prayer. As I began to yield control and to beg for mercy, God's response was swift: I was stripped of everything I had and of everyone I knew.

Remarkable as it sounds, I soon found myself far from my home in the east and stranded in an area of the Rocky Mountains so remote it was not on a map. I was a single mom, penniless, homeless, unemployed, clueless, and knuckleheaded. (To get the attention of a knucklehead you sometimes need a two-by-four.) My prayers got God's attention; now He wanted mine. In a nutshell, He wanted me to meet Someone—His Son.

On Christmas Eve of 1979 my boy and I had two toothbrushes, a backgammon game, and a big quilt. We had a diet pop and a can of tuna but no can opener. Our broken-down van sat next to the tiny log cabin a kindly minister had found for us. And we were in the middle of a snowstorm.

On Christmas Day of 1979 I searched the van on my knees to find sunflower seeds we might have dropped on our long drive cross-country, hoping I could find something to feed my son. That day, people who called themselves Christians knocked on the door to that cabin and whisked us to dinner. That same day, a knock came on another door, the door to my heart.

Shortly after Christmas I stood in a snow-crusted field. Cold as it was, the sun warmed my face as I looked at the sky and cried out again, "Whoever You are, whatever You are—help!" It is an astonishing and somewhat humorous story how help came.

Weeks later my son gave his life to Christ. The rest, as they say, is history, as the door to my heart flung wide open—I'd met Jesus.

Frankly, I don't know what I "became" at first. God the Holy Spirit might have begun churning in my heart, but I was a long way from joining anything or from even knowing what was happening to me. Peace did come, but to say this period of churning brought serenity to my heart or that I was hit by thunderclap and fell to my knees shouting "Alleluia" would be a stretch. When I look back, I see how and why I became a Christian, but for the life of me I can't tell you when. (What staggers my mind about the whole thing is that God heard me, loved me, and cherished me when I was rejecting Him.)

I began to read the Bible. Leave it to me to zero in on the one verse in the entire book that could trip me up. The second half of one sentence—from Jesus Himself!—in the Sermon on the Mount positively floored me: "Anyone who marries the divorced woman commits adultery" (Matthew 5:32).[1] Oh great. I was toast. Whether because of my dumb luck or the enemy of my soul I don't know, but I do know that because of that verse I felt doomed to singleness or to living a life apart from the body of Christ. Time, study, sound counsel, and prayer banished that thinking, and before long Jesus became central in my life. I grasped His hand more than 25 years ago and have never let go. To know Christ is to have your heart pierced, to want only to rest in His peace, to yearn to know Him more.

That I do not emulate Him and appropriate His words into my daily life as I should is part mystery and part human conundrum. I may fail at His commands, I may make a bad showing of His image, I may sometimes even become petulant and stomp my foot, but I cannot turn away because to do so is unthinkable.

Why We Turn to God When Things Go Wrong

"There are times when you hear that 'God never puts you through more than you can handle,' and you think, *How does He know how much I can take? I feel like I'm at a breaking point right now!*"

Shane

I wrote earlier that I do not believe God brings tragedy to us. That He allows it cannot be denied. Listen to King David's cry in Psalm 10: "Why, O LORD, do you stand far off? Why do you hide yourself in times of trouble?...But you, O God, do see trouble and grief; you consider it to take it in hand. The victim commits himself to you; you are the helper of the fatherless."

And now listen to the words of some single moms:

"Psalms written three thousand years ago show the same despair. This is the human condition, to be 'exhausted by it all,' and yet we keep going. We keep singing, even!"

"He is my air, food, water, everything. My all in all."

"For the most part my beliefs are stronger. You have to have something to depend on and believe in or the weight of it all would be too much."[2]

For some people this is counterintuitive. How can loss or pain turn someone to the very God who is allowing the suffering?

Let's use your children for a little help in understanding. Suppose your two children are playing outside. Though you monitor them through the kitchen window, you could be on a rocket ship to Mars and they wouldn't miss you, engaged as they are with play. One child gets stung by a bee. What happens?

"Momeeeeeee!" Frightened, in pain, and crying, the child dashes to you, calls to you, and needs you.

Again, listen to David: "Hear my prayer, O Lord; listen to my cry for mercy. In the day of my trouble I will call to you, for you will answer me" (Psalm 86:6-7).

The Bible tells us that man was designed by God for relationship with Him. Oh, sure, many of us have rejected this communion—or think we have—but it's there just the same. This yearning is so deeply imbedded, so much a part of us, that we run crying when we are in pain or trouble. God rejoices when we turn to Him.

Think of a bee sting. When your children get stung, where do you want them to run? To the neighbors? Of course not. You want them to come to you. You would be devastated if they went running to the lady across the street.

Magnify this response infinitely and try to wrap your mind around a God who is way past our ability to even understand but who says that He is our Father, that we are His children, that He loves us, and that He cares when we get stung.

God Is Just

Maybe you're all right with the Father thing, but you reject a bully of a God who exacts punishment and orders whole nations wiped out. You're just not into that kind of God. Well, sorry—this is just a smoke screen.

Some people are quick to find an escape clause, a reason for their rebellion and for their rejection. When I rejected God as a young woman, my retort was pretty common. "I don't believe in a God who would…" (Fill in the blank. I'm sure you have your ready response.)

We spend so much time justifying ourselves and are so self-absorbed that we start creating God in an image we are most comfortable with. Let's go back to the kids in the yard.

Standing there at the window, hands in soapy water, your eyes get as big as frying pans as you watch your nine-year-old daughter deliberately hit her brother with a broom handle. What happens? You just yawn and continue washing the dishes, right? In a pig's eye! You march out and perform a little triage, and after you make sure your son is still breathing you turn your full attention to the daughter who knows better. She's heard the rules a thousand times: No hitting, family members love each other, if you have a problem come to Mommy, on and on. You have raised your daughter in love, and you have not only enforced the no-hitting rule all her life, you've written these rules and taped them to the fridge. Yet she exhibits malicious behavior. You not only dispense punishment promptly but also demand an apology and restitution. It's called justice.

Let's go outside the family:

- Your library book is way overdue, and you pay a hefty fine.
- A man gets pinched for going 50 mph in a 35 mph zone. The speeding ticket exacts a steep penalty.

- A gunman opens fire in a store and kills many innocent people. Society demands justice.
- An entire village is massacred by warring tribes, and the world screams for justice.

Justice prevails. Yet when God is the One dispensing justice, we flip out. Especially if we are the ones wielding the broom.

Let's go a little further with the kids and pick on your son for a while. Let's say he's a pretty hip four-year-old. He refuses to obey you. "One," you say, looking him square in the eyes. "Two," you say, your voice threatening. You even add, "I mean it, Buster!" But he defies you. Your hand is called: "Three!" He does not comply. Justice is meted: "Off to your room!"

Let's add a 12-year-old son to this mix. You've warned that boy countless times he will miss the bus if he dawdles, but he calls your bluff every single day. He knows you'll take him to school. After all, you have to go to work, and he sure can't stay home alone.

Ignoring your wake-up calls, he misses the bus. What a surprise when Grandpa comes for the day to "babysit" and police the no-TV or electronic equipment rule. That kid stubbornly resisted learning you meant business when you wrote the rules. You had no choice but to stand by and to let him suffer the consequence of his rebellion.

Stick with me because here comes the best part. Your two children are playing outside. One child commits an act of violence against the other. Which child do you love more? "Neither!" you shout. Oh.

Praying to a Merciful God

As unfathomable as God is (justice and all), He wants only to have a relationship with His children. Once that resonates with us, faith is not too hard to muster. Crawl into the arms of your just and merciful God and say, *Whoever You are, whatever You are, help!* My hunch is that He will answer your prayer as swiftly as He answered the one I prayed in that snow-crusted field so long ago.

A verse from Jeremiah is commonly quoted because it brings hope and assurance to us all: " 'For I know the plans I have for you,' declares the LORD, 'plans to prosper you and not to harm you, plans to give you hope and a future.'" That is hope enough! But read on—listen to what comes next: "Then you will call upon me and come and pray to me, and I will listen to you. You will seek me and find me when you seek me with all your heart" (Jeremiah 29:11-13). Tack a rather important little factoid onto that verse—the fact that God does not lie—and you have a mighty big promise.

Prayer includes conversing with God, communing with God, worshipping God, submitting to God, thanking God, and petitioning God. It is a natural expression from the creature to the Creator. Prayer purifies our motives. Prayer is a critical part of our relationship to God; prayer *is* relationship!

The apostle Paul tells us to pray without ceasing. If you believe, as I do, that God the Holy Spirit superintended Paul when he wrote those words, then God Himself is telling us to pray all the time. Do you know what that means? It means that we are meant to commune with God in personal relationship.

Prayer Is Not a Charm

Some of us may have developed the idea that prayer is going before a celestial Santa Claus with a wish list. "Gimme this" or "gimme that" has become the general theme of prayer. We can accidentally foster this attitude in little children during our nighttime prayer routine. We want kids to understand and believe they have a faithful God who cares about His children, but unless checked, the "gimme litany" can begin at an early age. Prayer is much more than self-gain. To understand prayer better we should turn to Jesus.

Jesus is our supreme example for prayer. The gospel accounts tell us that Jesus prayed privately, prayed for others, and prayed for His own strength in time of trouble. He spent the entire night in prayer before He picked His apostles, told us to pray for those who mistreat us, and even taught us how to pray through the Lord's Prayer:

This, then, is how you should pray:
"Our Father in heaven,
   hallowed be your name,
   your kingdom come,
   your will be done
      on earth as it is in heaven.
Give us today our daily bread.
Forgive us our debts,
      as we also have forgiven our debtors.
And lead us not into temptation,
but deliver us from the evil one" (Matthew 6:9-13).

The prayer example Jesus gave starts off with praise and is immediately followed by submission: God's will be done. Someone once told me he could not understand why Christians had to submit to God. Why couldn't they just be in charge of themselves? The suggestion was that Christians were nitwits who couldn't make a real decision. Let's look at it another way.

If a Creator God really does exist, a sovereign Being, a just and merciful Father, wouldn't He who knows everything in time and space know what is best for us? How insolent for us to suggest that we with our limited, finite brains could make better decisions for ourselves than God can. Christians want to be submitted to God's will! This doesn't make us robots; this makes us earnest to be obedient and ever seeking the grace of God and direction of the Holy Spirit.

The next part of Jesus' prayer asks for our daily provision. It does not paraphrase into "give me this day everything my heart could possibly want, O Lord." It asks for today's needs. (God deals in one-day-at-a-time counsel big time!) Jesus cautions His followers to seek spiritual values and to put their trust in God for temporal needs.

A significant part of this prayer is the last sentence: "Deliver us from the evil one." We should pray for spiritual protection daily. If children are in our care, we must pray for their protection. Before I open my eyes each day I pray for everyone close to me—even our homes and pets! I pray for protection from ourselves, from others, and from the Evil One.

Prayer is dialogue with a personal God. We do not control God through our prayer. Remember? His will be done, not ours. Neither is prayer a monologue, a monotonous appeal from our lips to God's ears. Prayer is dialogue, a two-way communication. We hear from God through the hope we nurture in our hearts, through the Scriptures, by the answers we receive, and by the still small voice in our souls.

Family Prayer

In addition to praying for your family, do you pray with them? Have you created in your children a concept of God that makes Him understandable and as easy to reach as picking up a phone?

Teach your children to pray. Pray with them. Help them to express themselves in prayer. Encourage them to turn to prayer for decisions they face in their life, especially decisions that affect their ethical and moral behavior. Teach them that prayer is a time of praise. Softly sing a hymn. Bring reverence back to prayer; it will be good discipline for both you and your children.

> *A Bedtime Prayer*
> *Before in sleep I close my eyes,*
> *To Thee, O God, my thoughts arise*
> *To thank Thee for Thy blessings all,*
> *Which come to us, Thy children small.*
> *O keep me safe throughout the night,*
> *That I may see the morning light.*
> Source unknown

Many mothers share prayer with their children at meals and at bedtime. Depending on how many children you have, bedtime can be a zoo; praying with each child may be unrealistic. Meals are often the best chance to say something meaningful. Many families use the dinner table as a forum for prayer and conversation. (Others blurt through repetitious grace before meals that sounds more like belching than blessings.)

I know mothers who would not think of sending their children to school without laying hands on their heads in blessing. One mother prays in the car as she takes the kids to school.

If you have a liturgical or traditional background, you may be more comfortable with formatted prayer and may be unfamiliar with impromptu conversation with God. Please remember, God wants to hear from you. Talk to Him.

> "Church is the perfect place for imperfect people."
>
> *Marcie*

Church

Debbye has strong words about church: "Never make church optional, beginning at birth. I never did. When they are on their own, they can make that decision for themselves. When they live under your roof, you have the right to make that decision. Find a church they had a part in choosing...one they can enjoy."

You may believe fully in God, and you may have experienced new life through Christ, yet perhaps you steadfastly stay clear of any building marked "church." Many women have just reason to stay clear of church, which has been to them a place of marginalization, of pain, of stern finger-wagging, of guilt, or of shame. I wouldn't go to a place like that either.

Just like marriages, churches are made up of people, and people aren't perfect. As Marcie said, "Church is the perfect place for imperfect people." Countless single mothers have found solace in their faith and have clung to their church family, but listen to a summary about church attendance by a single mother in Texas:

> You know you want to set an example for your children and bring them up knowing God. The problem is...you have to find the right church because unfortunately you will find such "righteous" people who believe

because you are a single parent you are beyond God's love. They treat you like you have a disease, which is a shame because a lot of single moms skip church for this reason.

How wonderful it would be if I could point at random to any local church and know that a single mother could find support there. The church has fallen short in this regard and seldom offers help for single moms in spite of the biblical admonition that orders the care of widows and children as paramount. "Religion that God our Father accepts as pure and faultless is this: to look after orphans and widows in their distress" (James 1:27). I don't see how the divorced or abandoned mother is different from the widowed mom.

Many women who have suffered from the shattering experience of a broken marriage have found hope and wholeness in Christ. Turning to Him has brought these women to church pews on Sunday morning, and the church must respond with compassion to these women and their children.

We seem more interested in castigating women for what they did in the bedroom than offering them a helping hand, regardless of Christ's example to the contrary. We appear to want everyone else to be "pure and faultless." This has got to change. The role of the local church is critical in any child's life, but it may be a life preserver in the case of fatherless or motherless children. The congregants of every church should know which children in their membership are without fathers (or mothers) and see that they have routine fatherly representation. Possibilities are limitless, from seniors acting as grandfathers, to younger men taking the children on outings or teaching skills that will equip them for life. This is not only a suggestion for men and boys either. As I stated in the last chapter, girls need mature men in their lives every bit as much as boys do. Needless to say, any surrogate relationship must be carefully screened to protect children from abuse.

Churches can provide more help than just healthy modeling for boys and girls. Moms need help. I will never forget an early morning scene at a bakery in Virginia. A young African-American woman studied an economics text while her two young children fidgeted nearby. A single mom, she'd come to the bakery with her children for warmth. She studied fervently before her college class...and before she could bring her children to free child care when Head Start opened. Joe and I offered our grandparent services and occupied the children until the time for the woman to leave. How I wished I could have offered to care for her children—without charge—while she attended class. Something like this would be an incalculably valuable service for a single mother. Today's churches are filled with older men and women who have time for bridge and golf while mothers like the woman in the bakery live in desperation. This ought not to be.

> *"A father to the fatherless, a defender of widows, is God in his holy dwelling. God sets the lonely in families" (Psalm 68:5-6).*

Single mothers carry the immense responsibility of training up their children and are the spiritual heads of their families. It is a tough task. I recommend that single mothers prayerfully ask the Father to the fatherless to bring them to a church with supportive friendships that can ease their load.

A good church is out there for you. Let's appropriate some of the Sermon on the Mount: Seek and ye shall find.

Children and Church

Don't deny your children spiritual education or nurturing. A popular contemporary notion is to let children decide about God by themselves. Make no mistake—a personal decision to accept or reject Jesus Christ faces every informed person on the planet. Yet we say to children, in effect, "This is one big, scary, hard world, but grow up and figure it out for yourself, kiddo." This is borderline abusive.

Of eight teenagers interviewed for a newspaper report on children and church, seven responded positively about religious services.[3] One 17-year-old commented, "I'm happy my parents made me go, giving me a seed from which to grow my faith."

We hope kids go to church because they feel they are part of the body of Christ. Children should be fully integrated into church for their own sense of community and for the value they offer the adult community.

The contributions of youth ministers are outstanding and vitally important, but we must be careful not to segregate children from the vibrancy of the body of Christ. We invest significant time, energy, and money into stimulating and entertaining children, making church fun. Why are we so determined to make all of life stimulating and fun for children? This can make for shallow people and play a role in poor character development.

As I will reiterate in chapter 9, much is at stake when children are not acquainted with Jesus Christ, biblical teaching, and church attendance. The souls of our children are at stake. Add to that the quality of their lives, including a strong foundation for adulthood, their contributions to society, the vitality of the church, and finally, the future of the church. (Show me a church with no children and I'll show you a dying church.)

We need to commit as a body to become stewards of our children, to revitalize children's programs, and to strategize to make modifications that create kid-friendly and integrative environments.

Spiritual Exercises

- Keep prayer short if young children are involved. Their attention span is about 17 seconds long!

- Don't pressure a child to pray out loud. Encourage, yes—pressure, no.

- Always have Bibles handy. Children and teens should have Bibles that fit their level of maturity.

- Keep a prayer journal. A spiral notebook will do, and each child can decorate his or her own. The journal can be corporate, for the entire family, or it can be highly personal, which means highly confidential. Older children can write their own messages to the Lord, and younger children can dictate to Mom or siblings. Prayer journals can be highly effective in communicating with the Lord.

- Encourage youngsters to be aware of the result of prayer in their lives. Keep a chart or list of answered prayer—yes or no!

- Kids love stories. A mom can pray to the Lord about the child's day, taking an average day and adding thanksgivings and blessings and humor. Ad lib a prayer and personify it for the child. A youngster will be wide-eyed with feelings of importance.

- Children should learn that some prayer can be expressed in song. Teach them a favorite old hymn, and talk about the meaning of the words. Write a hymn together.

- Write a special prayer to use before meals.

- Write special holiday prayers.

- Ask capable children to give one-minute sermons explaining what they have just read in the Bible. Our son used to do this and said some pretty sensible stuff.

- Act out Scripture.

- Read a Bible story and interview the characters and witnesses, using your children. Use your imagination. Record these interviews on tape or on a computer. Children love to hear recordings of themselves.

- Put Scripture and prayer into action by involving your family in Christian service to others in the community. Don't just talk about the hungry and the homeless and the poor and the shut-ins. Do something about them.

RESOURCES

Awana clubs are age-specific and geared for children. Clear, consistent presentation of the gospel is a hallmark of Awana club meetings, as are Bible memory, games, and an evangelistic focus. (United States: 630-213-2000, Canada: 905-892-5252, www.awanayouth.com)

Bible Study Fellowship is an interdenominational lay Christian organization with Bible study classes in cities across the United States and the world. They offer classes during the day for women and classes during the evening for men, for women, and for single young adults (ages 18–35). Bible Study Fellowship also offers a children's program. (United States: 1-877-273-3228 [toll free], outside the United States: 1-210-492-4676 [not toll free], www.bsfinternational.org)

Kids 4 Truth International provides local church children's programs that strive to teach boys and girls 120 of the most important truths of Scripture in an understandable, useful, and memorable way. (clubs.kids4truth.com)

READING

Steve Grissom and Kathy Leonard, *Through a Season of Divorce: Devotions for Healing from Separation and Divorce* (Nashville: Thomas Nelson, 2005).

Stormie Omartian, *The Power of a Praying Woman* (Eugene, OR: Harvest House Publishers, 2002).

Richard Foster, *Prayer: Finding the Heart's True Home* (New York: HarperCollins, 1992).

C.S. Lewis, *The Case for Christianity* (New York: Collier Books, 1989).

N.T. Wright, *The Challenge of Jesus* (Downers Grove, IL: InterVarsity Press, 1999).

John R. Stott, *The Cross of Christ* (Downers Grove, IL: InterVarsity Press, 1986).

Joe White and Jim Weidmann, *Lead Your Teen to a Lifelong Faith* (Colorado Springs: Focus on the Family Publishing, 2005).

Five

Finding Time for It All

"Personal time? You gotta be kidding!
Maybe take a quick shower, brush my teeth,
and slap on makeup so I don't scare anyone."

Marcie

I presume by now you have abandoned your quest for perfection. I have a hunch that time and stress have chewed you up and spit you out a time or two. I have a hunch you often feel as if you're juggling bowling balls (and have been bonked in the head!). I know exactly what you are going through. No, really…my months on end as grandmother in residence for our son and daughter-in-law's three small children have given me a lot more than bonding experience. They have put me in an environment where balancing routine and life is a challenging task, and they have opened my eyes to the phenomenon Al Gore once called "the time deficit in family life."

Parents commonly run themselves into zombielike states of

93

fatigue and strain as they try to get things done. Make that a single parent—particularly a single mom—and watch the hours disappear as fast as a bowl of bonbons.

Jennifer is the mother of five children under 14. I expected her answer to the question of time to be typical. She surprised me: "I used to run myself ragged, but I let go of that because it didn't bring God glory."

Navigating Time

Why do people talk of time as an enemy? Time is part of God's created order. It is the substance of our day; it is a gift. Yet time is more than the hours of each day; it is weeks and months and seasons. It is sunrise and sunset; it is stages of life. It is waiting in expectation for the birth of a child, for Christmas Eve, for summer vacation. It is also your place in history, where God has put you in this moment, when you are called to live according to His purpose.

You say you're pressed for time, call time your mortal enemy, panic as time flies, and pout glumly as time ticks by. You could not cram one more thing into your busy life before you fall into an exhausted heap each night. This is not a good thing.

Come with me to the banks of the Swan River in Bigfork, Montana, to a section of river called the Wild Mile. If you stand near a small, squat dam, you can look one way and see water so calm, nary a ripple is in sight. A bridge spans the river there, and fishermen languorously pitch their lines. The bridge is necessary to get to the other side, and though still, the waters underneath are thick with tree stumps and ragged rocks.

Close to Glacier National Park, the glacial bed of the Swan River is bumpy with boulders. This is apparent if you turn and look the other way toward the Wild Mile. Water crashes on the river with force that flips its covers back and exposes its bed as a perilous place. I have crossed the river on days when its thunder dims to a low growl, carefully stepping through shallow pools of water, alongside and over jutted rock.

Though the water on the Wild Mile is always threatening, in some seasons its fury is more pronounced and seemingly boundless, such as spring runoff or after a period of heavy rain. People have died trying to navigate the Wild Mile.

Why do I tell you this? Because I'm talking about your life.

You are standing on the bank of a river called Single Mother. Your task is to get from one side of the river to the other without falling in and getting your gear wet. Too wide to jump over, you are forced to study the river and to think hard. Just where should you cross? While you evaluate the river, look for telltale signs: Do the rocks you plan to step on have sturdy foundations, or will they wobble sideways? Are they covered with ice crystals, slime, or wet moss? Are jutted logs or stumps covered with rotted bark that will send you bottom side down into the frenetic water? Is a bridge nearby?

Bridges give you a chance to walk confidently for a while. From a bridge you can peer into the river to appreciate its beauty, you can look at the surrounding countryside, or you can soak in the sound of birds and bugs. Bridges give your spirit a chance to soar, even if you face more peril before you hit your destination. The dry bank—the other side...your bed—is only a few yards away.

Your *bed?* Yep. Think of each day, morning to night, from the perspective of one single task: to get to the other side. Some days you will find yourself submerged up to your neck, some days fighting rapids, some days sailing on still waters. On some days you will find time to rest or picnic on a bridge; some days you will run breathlessly over sure, strong planks. Every now and then you may catch your toe on a plank and fall—*splat*—in the center of your safe place. But your resolve must never waver because the other side is in sight. Besides, staying on your morning riverbank is too risky; the morning bank on this river washes away and deposits you in swirling water. Wake up without good footing and you're going to career down the bank, bouncing like oil in a hot wok. Standing still is not an option. Neither is reckless or indifferent demeanor: Wild dives or cannonballs into this river will split your head open like a coconut. And woe to you if you decide to stay put halfway across. All sorts of troubles can come to a marooned mom sitting on a pointy rock in the middle of churning water.

There is another compelling reason for you to get to the other side: Your kids beat you there. They're waiting for you to tuck them in. And the bottom line is this: Nobody else can.

In the morning your children will wake up hungry, needing their hair combed, and too foolish to wear proper clothes on cold days. At all times they will need to be held and hugged and protected. Every day. All the time. One crossing at a time.

So every morning when you awaken, before you open your eyes, pray this prayer: *Lord, I am depending on You to get me to the other side of today with as few rapids as possible. Just this day, just this day, make the waters still today.*

Why Are We Adrift?

One reason we are adrift is because tomorrow even exists. There is more to tomorrow than meets the eye. We've already glimpsed tomorrow's devastating impact on our anxieties and heard from Jesus to just take care of today, please. What else is there? Answer this: How many times have you told yourself you would get to something tomorrow? Consider one never-ending and miserable chore: the laundry.

Your laundry routine is going well until you hit the Saturday morning lazies and just feel like lounging in bed. Nothing wrong with that. Rather than doing the wash a bit later, though, you tell yourself you will catch up tomorrow. But tomorrow is Sunday, and you know how hectic Sunday mornings are. Besides, you truly do try to rest on Sunday. Well, maybe Monday. But getting everyone geared up for the week, motivating yourself...you'll do laundry when you get home—or tomorrow for sure. Now laundry becomes a production:

The sheets should be washed, the dirty clothes are cloning themselves in the hamper, and you are beset by the idea of the wash after a long day of work. It will hold until tomorrow. Tomorrow morning you feel punky, coming down with that darn cold that's been going around. Everything can wait, including the laundry that has now transmogrified into the blob that ate Detroit. Tomorrow, tomorrow. Sooner or later, tomorrow turns into today with a whale of a load of laundry to do. Tomorrow breeds procrastination.

Procrastination

When you procrastinate, you create stress for yourself, and (as was demonstrated with the laundry) you often create more work. This is a no-brainer: Do what you can to banish procrastination and persevere in a plenitudious preponderance of perfectly pleasurable pastimes.

As a single mother you've no doubt learned that you cannot afford to procrastinate. You may have learned that you can do things in a timely manner. A good trick to enable this is to break your task into frames, just as you are coping with life in smaller frames rather than looking at the big picture. Let's go back to the laundry.

Team Laundry: The Big, Ugly Picture

When it comes to laundry, as my mom would say, "You make too much work for yourself!" Look at this issue through the lens of time management.

Some clothes that have been worn yet are perfectly clean end up in the hamper. Why? Not because of a national mandate to never wear clothes more than once (this is actually true of some cultures) but because you and your children do not put perfectly clean clothes where they belong. So you wash way more clothes than necessary. You are trading one split second's effort to hang or put away clothes for hauling, sorting, washing, drying, folding, hauling, and putting away. Am I the only one who thinks this is insane?

Wash time. You cram the washer, which means clothes get "sort of" washed and poorly rinsed. Then you cram the dryer. You rarely clean the lint trap. The dryer (and the trap) are so full that the cycle ends with clothes in a massive damp ball. This ball of clothes ends up permanently wrinkled. You have also created a serious fire hazard by not emptying that lint trap, and you have most certainly paid more in utilities because the washer and dryer had to work extra hard.

Still with me? Once you take your clothes out of the dryer, you schlep them to the living room couch to fold. This folding gets interrupted for an assortment of reasons, and during such interruptions the children (or the spaniel) come along and undo all your efforts. Once the folding is finally finished, you put severely wrinkled clothes into that black hole where you keep your ironing, never, ever to be seen again. You then put all the folded clothes in a basket and carry this basket to the bedrooms, where you sometimes put the clothes away. If you do not put them away, the clothes basket becomes more handy than the hamper, and soon dirty clothes are piling on top of the clean, all to be carted downstairs and washed again. You actually know you are rewashing clean clothes, but you do so anyway.

Your bed sheets have not been changed for so long you could grow mushrooms in there, but the notion of stripping beds (especially those bunk beds!) is enough to make you faint from fatigue. This, along with the gargantuan task of daily laundry, causes you to wish you lived on a tropical island in a tank top and a fig leaf.

Team Laundry: The Small, Easy Frames

Laundry accumulates for a family with children, so you vow to stay on top of it with a daily load. The daily wash becomes as routine as your morning coffee. You and the kids grab clothes as you head out of your bedrooms and plop them in the washer. This takes less than one minute and is incorporated in the trip from bedroom to kitchen. You usually throw a towel or two in the washer to make the expense of running the load worthwhile. Before you leave for the day, you put the clothes in the dryer on a time setting that will fully dry (not fry) your clothes. This task takes perhaps ten seconds. You know towels slow down drying, but you're a single mom, not Heloise. (Delicates are culled and hung to air dry.) Sometime in the evening you take the clothes out of the dryer, glad to have permanent press and wrinkle-resistant clothing during this time of your life. You banned dry cleaning, linen, and 100 percent cotton years ago.

You take the clean clothes from the dryer directly to where they actually "live." Children who are old enough have learned to smooth clothing with their hands and to fold or roll their clothes. You all fold and put clothes into their "parking place." (More on where clothes go later in this chapter.)

You have a designated "sheets day." Top sheets usually go a couple weeks before changing; bottom sheets and pillow cases need weekly washing. Each person strips his or her bed and immediately puts on a clean sheet since you have two sheet sets and two pillowcases for each bed. Once washed, next week's sheets go into their designated parking place, a lidded bin under each bed.

When you are daunted by the big picture, a simple chore that might take minutes often turns into the equivalent of a meat cleaver hanging over your head as minutes escalate into hours. This is a good time to remember that tomorrow never comes. It is also a good time not to give tomorrow short shrift.

*Tomorrow I will do/be*_____

_____

*In order to do/be that, today I will*____

_____

Respect Tomorrow, Live Today

If you've read any of my previous books, you know I encourage a healthy respect for the future. We need goals, and we need plans to reach those goals. By all means, think about who you want to be tomorrow and what you hope to accomplish. Go ahead and dream. Dreams are the stuff of hope whether they come true or not.

But everything changes when you become a single mom. Rules change because life is different for you. Long-range goals are still essential, but the emphasis has to change. You need to focus on one goal above all others: getting to the other side of the river. Use *only* today to accomplish your goals and dreams.

Why else are we adrift and unable to find enough time in our day? We get distracted, we lack expertise, we lack routine, and we are lazy.

Distractions

Distractions come in countless forms: interruptions from you, from others, from technology; weather, accidents, or mechanical breakdowns; illness, unexpected demands on your time. It's called life, Mom. Life happens. When life gets in the way of living, it takes away the time you planned to use for something else. Let's examine a few of the distractions that come our way.

The Distraction of You

One distraction takes your time ruthlessly: you. We manage to disrupt our days all by ourselves. Whether we misuse time by being a vivacious personality who talks the time away, by being a poor self-motivator who justifies the time away, or by being scattered and unfocused, it all boils down to self-sabotage. Yet the whine goes on: *I'm running ragged, I don't have any time!* Look to yourself first.

The Distraction of Others

Your phone's ringing...your neighbor wants to chat...your daughter is whining and demanding your attention even though you spent the better part of this morning with her...your coworker wants to jaw about work conditions...your mother is in a snit because you are not responding to her e-mail. You are glued to the TV because of a carjacking taking place on the news channel in real time. Any of this sound familiar? All of it.

The message of chapter 3 was that single mothers need other people in their lives, but a slight variation to this theme is that to manage your day well, you have to wisely engage others to your advantage. It is not to your advantage if you allow other people to march into your day and to usurp time without your permission. Unplanned interruptions can gobble time we need for pressing matters.

On the other hand, we are social beings and do not live in a vacuum. I've met some people who carry privacy to extremes, hurting those who need or want relationships. A conversation with your neighbor may be more important than the chore at hand; time with your daughter may be a necessary comfort to an unusually needy child; answering your mother's e-mail just plain makes good sense.

If others seek your company, they do so because they love you, respect your advice, enjoy your company...or they are pains in the neck. Communicate your time constraints to any offenders. Explain your circumstance without issuing fiats or ultimatums. Be cordial. For denser folk you may have to be clearer: "This is not a good time for me...I am much too busy to talk right now...I must get back to work."

Do *not* say you will get back to the pesty person or tell him or her to get back to you at a different time. If you do, you will put undue pressure on yourself. If you suggest the person call you another time, you are prolonging the inevitable showdown when you have to announce you haven't time for incessant chatter and interruption.

The Distraction of Technology

Technology that was designed to make our lives simpler has instead enslaved us and detached us from others. Technology has obscured or obliterated our interconnectedness and has become a nasty taskmaster. We rush to every ring, beep, and buzz. We feed machines, empty machines, and try to keep machines running smoothly. We feel pressure to answer the latest batch of e-mails that have sprung up overnight like dandelions. Still we obediently equip ourselves with pagers and cell phones. We can't get away.

Technology has also erased our need to learn some skills. A big reason for our lack of time organization is our lack of skills. (Organized people have little problem with time.) We lack skills because we never learned skills. We never learned skills partly because the cord between generations has been slashed. Children once learned at their grandmother's knee through observation and from her counsel and discipline. Daughters once learned from a mother's model. Sons once learned from a father's model. Well, good luck, duck! Grandma is tucked away in a nursing home or out on the golf course, and Mom and Dad are on the 5:30 train from work. Kids aren't even home to learn, staying late for play practice, running late from slinging burgers at the fast-food joint, or killing time at a friend's over a video game. Our seams have ripped. Anything moms or dads learned from their parents has been consigned to nostalgia or lost altogether. Children now learn for themselves or from the home and garden network.

Part of the loss of skills is the result of technological evolution. From automatic dishwashers to vacuums that clean by themselves to computer chips in cars that print out precise mechanical malfunctions, many machines have replaced our need for skills.

The skills I'm talking about go beyond repair and maintenance. I'm talking about hands-on common sense, resourcefulness, a determination to succeed or persevere, and a work ethic that includes elbow grease and a willing spirit.

Lack of Routine

If you are racing the clock and running like a chicken without a head with no normative standards in your week, you need routine. Time moves more slowly when it follows a routine or rhythm. From all I've read, children thrive on routine. I know I do. There is much to be said about spontaneity, and may it never leave our lives! Spontaneity is waking the kids at 6:30 AM and driving to a hilltop to watch the sunrise, dancing together in your pajamas, pledging to eat a healthy breakfast tomorrow but having banana splits for dinner tonight.

But routine anchors and stabilizes us. Routine glues our days together. It can become a godsend in our day. Having a routine timeline for most days, especially school and work days, aids immeasurably in managing your day. You manage your day by managing your time.

Laziness

I simply cannot find any way around this. We seem to be a culture desperate for excuses to liberate us from either guilt or the slightest suggestion we may be flawed. We are raising our children with this mind-set when we gush over every single thing they do and dare not present criticism, constructive as it may be. We want everything sugarcoated.

We create whole organizations around our inability to accept responsibility for our actions. A trend of "anonymous" groups have cropped up to service this thinking. They follow the unparalleled example of Alcoholics Anonymous.

Alcoholism is a disease; support groups are invaluable for people battling dependency, and I am all for such groups. But something like Messy People Anonymous? Please. Stop looking for justification for your laziness. Certainly, inertia can come from depression. If depression is severe, please seek counsel. But in general, some of us are just plain lazy. Incidentally, sloth, or laziness, is counted among the seven deadly sins.

Time to Spare

We find time for that which is important to us. The problem is not that we have too little time; how we manage time is the issue. Again, to manage our day we must manage our time. Focus on today, please!

I've learned a few lessons about time. For one, the more I do, the more time I seem to have. Yes, I've held hand to forehead and gone through swooning motions, acting as if I was positively swamped. Truth be told, I was looking for acknowledgment of my hard work.

I have also learned something about time that seems counter-intuitive: When I slow down, time slows down. When I am in a frenzy, I am more apt to run amok. When I slow down, I am more calculated, methodical, and peaceful. This is often when I am most productive.

(By "slowing down" I do not mean being habitually late. Chronic lateness shows not only lack of time management but also lack of respect. By slowing down I mean decompressing, "chilling" a bit. Attitude plays a huge role here.)

Can someone bite off more than she can chew? Yes. If you are a single mother of quadruplets (I know of one), then you probably don't have enough hours in the day, though I suspect you have such an effective routine that you accomplish more than many mothers. You have no choice but to dig deeply and to cope. Those children have to be fed, burped, and changed.

Undeniably, some circumstances do prevail that put us at odds with time, such as working more than one job or having a child with disabilities. But generally we are treading water up to our necks because we never learned to swim.

To manage your day, you have to look at 24 hours in a new light. Actually, you would do well to turn off the light. Oh, what havoc the lightbulb brings! Once we slept when the day turned dark, recharging our bodies, giving our organs a chance to detoxify and rejuvenate, and giving our bones a rest from gravity. Now we flick a switch. We upset many natural rhythms of life with technology. When natural rhythms are upset, we are upset. With that in mind, we should look at ordering our days (not nights), and slash 24 hours to 16, allowing 8 hours of rest for you and your children.

The Pareto Time Principle promotes the notion that only 20 percent of what you do in a day really matters. By focusing on that 20 percent of your tasks that are really important, you not only work smart, you work smart on the right things. Here's rough paraphrase of the Pareto Time Principle: Prioritize.

The 16-Hour Day

See how easy this is? You only have to order 16 hours each day! Up to the task? Let's go.

Right off the bat, deduct nine hours for work and commute. (I'm writing under the assumption you have a job away from home.) That leaves seven hours. Deduct one hour each for breakfast and dinner. (Way more than you need.) You now have to manage a net of five hours. That's much easier to handle.

What can you do with five hours each day? You've already done the wash, remember?

Time Wise

"Don't go empty-handed!" When we were young, this was one of my mother's mantras. She constantly badgered us girls to haul something from the car if we were going into the house, to carry something upstairs if we were going to our rooms, to take the trash outside if we were headed that way. Mom was right. Not going empty-handed is one of the countless skills I've learned about using time wisely. To this day, I never go anyplace empty-handed.

Wise use of time also means learning to prioritize and to compromise, to not be fanatic. Ask yourself, *What matters most?* Do those things first.

Some time-wise matters in your day must be managed intelligently. A good example is recharging your cell phone. When can this best be accomplished? When the phone can be parked for a while—at night. (It recharges its battery while you recharge yours.)

To me, a critical component to time management—and therefore being time wise—is not making more work for yourself in the first place. Why are some children allowed the run of the house with free access to everything from every drawer and cupboard to Mom's pocketbook? The kids run rampant and take the house apart, and Mom feels overwhelmed to put it back together again—not to mention the time she now has to spend looking for the car keys Junior deposited in the box of oatmeal.

This is not only poor time management, it is poor parenting. While we are on this subject, when children are finished playing with their toys (various pots and pans included), they should be expected to put them away in an age-appropriate manner.

Time Sensitive

Create a master calendar. Enter all time-sensitive events and responsibilities so you can see them at a glance. Office supply stores sell big, year-at-a-glance desk calendars. This calendar will become your list of everything you must do in a timely manner. Always have your master calendar in an easily accessible spot. A desk is great if clutter will not accumulate on top. The refrigerator is best if you purchase heavy-duty clasp magnets. Attach a pencil to one of the magnets with a string. Flag all time-sensitive notations with red stars.

Yearly: Think about events such as birthdays, anniversaries, graduations, holidays, and other occasions that require advance planning, thought, or action.

Ongoing: Note appointments to make and keep, such as annual physicals, well-baby checkups, vet visits, dental appointments, legal meetings, and parent-teacher conferences.

Monthly: Schedule times to pay your bills.

Time Attentive

This is where you start the process of goal setting. What issues need your attention soon but are not cause for grave concern if not handled promptly? Unless you are facing breakdowns, car and home maintenance come to mind, as well as vacations, school breaks and holidays, finances, and all administrative tasks. If your calendar has space, enter time-attentive issues at the beginning of each month. Look closely at your world: What needs attention when?

Time Constraints

When thinking about your day, you must factor events that are not subject to change. We already mentioned work and your commute. Consider your routine: What uses your time regularly? Do you volunteer at a co-op, attend class, visit someone regularly, participate in club meetings, or go to a Bible study? Do you watch a TV show faithfully every Tuesday night? Use a fat-tipped blue marker to highlight this time each day.

Time Out

Having a life of your own will help to make you a better parent. Time out is about play.

> "Play? You mean, like, fun? Put on loud praise music
> and dance your head off. Dance on your furniture
> just to spite your mother. I broke the spring
> in a couch once doing that."
>
> *Marcie*

I venture that apart from playing with their children, most single moms would show stunned confusion when asked if they play. Play can be as planned and structured as a vacation and as brief and spontaneous as a half-hour visit to a coffee shop. Listen to what some single mothers do for themselves:

"I soak. Candles, essential oil, music, a good book, and Barney bubble-bath."

"I enjoy sitting down to watch a chick flick with a can of cold pork 'n' beans. It's a ritual that brings me great comfort."

"I go to a local McDonald's all by myself and order the biggest bag of French fries they have. Sometimes I order two bags. I don't know whether it is the salt or the fat or the potassium, but I feel better after those fries."

"I go shopping for new underwear."

A Sample Day Planner: Day One

To-Do List

- ✓ **Time sensitive:** Children make Easter cards for grandparents
- ☐ Rent payment due
- ☐ Library books must be returned
- ☐ **Time attentive:** Lube, oil, filter car
- ☐ Look into more life insurance
- ☐ Start thinking about summer and what to do with the kids
- ☐ **Time constraints:** Staff meeting; work half-hour early
- ☐ Missy's tumbling class
- ☐ **Time out:** Walk with friend if sun holds out; shoot for 15 minutes of Pilates if it doesn't
- ☐ **Hope to do:** Clean one drawer in dresser
- ☐ Begin to knit tea cozy as part of birthday gift for friend
- ☐ Pick up around trash cans
- ☐ Start reading *The Lion, the Witch and the Wardrobe* with the children

This is all about routine. It is about looking at your master to-do list, considering time constraints in the day, factoring in time for yourself, and developing simple time management skills.

I suggest you have a loose plan to accomplish certain things and shoot for that plan every day.

A Sample Day Planner: Day Two

To-Do List

- ✓ **Time sensitive:** Mail Easter cards to grandparents
- ☐ Oops…return library books and pay fine
- ☐ Call neighbor to see if she can help care for children during summer
- ☐ **Time attentive:** Lube, oil, filter for car (maybe during lunch hour?)
- ☐ Check Internet to compare prices on term life insurance
- ☐ **Time constraints:** No extracurriculars for any of us
- ☐ **Time out:** Walk with friend again; do Pilates sometime today
- ☐ Pluck eyebrows and give myself a facial
- ☐ **Hope to do:** Clean one drawer in dresser
- ☐ Finish tea cozy
- ☐ Haul recycling
- ☐ Plant bulbs near trash can area

Organization

Organization is the foundation on which you build success. Organization of stuff will bring serenity to a hectic life, will bring order to your day, and will bring you time galore. You needn't go further than the home and garden channel to find shows dedicated to reducing clutter. The scene is always the same: An expert organizer visits the home of some bizarrely and proudly chaotic person, walks into a room stuffed with stuff and wails, "Oh, how can this be? I will help you. But first you have to help yourself. Get rid of most of this stuff." (The twist to organization for the single mom is that she usually lives in cramped quarters where space—especially storage space—is hard to come by.)

Now it's my turn to say it: Get rid of half of your stuff. Let me tell you why.

We have been taught that happiness and satisfaction come from things, and that is a lie. We are a culture cluttered from consumption. Consumption is neither good nor bad; it is necessary to live. The amount we consume is what gets us into trouble in our pocketbooks, in our pants size, and in the lack of order in our lives. And yet we keep bringing home more stuff.

Stop being a slave to all your stuff. Organize your world, pare down your stuff, and stop feeding this monster. Use what you have. An excellent sentiment goes like this: Happiness, peace, and satisfaction come from wanting what we have, not from getting what we want.

The best example I can give is that hammock of stuffed toys in your child's room. The hammock is so filled that furry little critters fall to the floor for lack of space. (More on this issue later.)

Maybe—*maybe*—the child plays with the stuffed toys on the top of the pile. The rest are permanently buried, never to be seen again, sort of like your ironing. This is wrong for a multitude of reasons, not the least being that every toy in that hammock cost money.

Clutter in our lives equals clutter in our emotions (stress) and clutter in our souls (lack of peace). Consider your clothes closet, consider the garage, consider your kitchen cupboards, and consider that ironing!

When I wrote about the laundry I mentioned two sets of sheets for each bed. No more, no less. I'd wager that right now many of you have linen closets so full and untidy you can hardly close the door, and the mystery of all this is that you will never use the stuff that is in there. And your dressers and closets...

Team Laundry Revisited: Putting Away Clothes

Even if you develop a smart laundry system that works well for you and your children, the lion's share of difficulty with laundry comes with putting it away when clean. Make this as easy as possible.

For the record, I am not a fan of dressers. I don't like anything that stacks clothes one on top of the other. Use the drawers for easy things like socks or underwear. If you do put shirts or pants in drawers, roll them and put them in the drawers side by side.

Without benefit of a dresser, a "sock drawer" or "underwear drawer" could be a simple wicker basket. If you stack clothes on a shelf, don't go too high, and use dividers to hold stacked clothes in place. Hang clothes neatly, install lower bars for children, and purchase children's clothes hangers for ease of use.

Consider a prefabricated compartmentalized shoe organizer for children's clothing. Roll pants, shirts, and sweatshirts neatly and put one or two to a box. Home improvement stores sell some that have as many as 20 compartments. Use a shoe bag hung on the back of the bedroom door for shoes and clothing.

Television as a Time Benefit

Though I've written rather tough indictments about television and have strong opinions about its misuse, it can be a blessing to the single mother's life. There is more than one reason for this, and it starts with tongue-in-cheek editorializing:

- The pundits who rant about children and TV may have never had a cranky child who is driving them up the wall in spite of excellent parenting. You may just need a break.
- The pundits may have never had a morning when they were fighting the flu and still had to care for youngsters.
- The pundits may have never had a time when work had to be done and TV filled in rather nicely as a babysitter.

To all of that, I say: What's wrong with that? What *is* wrong is overuse, misuse, and lack of parental monitoring. Turn off unnecessary television, and use the time for something that needs getting done. You might be surprised how much time this frees.

Just Say No

Every time management book I've studied has drummed home a common message: Just say no. Unless you are absolutely certain you can handle a job or absolutely want to take one on, do not volunteer for anything that will take valuable time from your routine. Pucker those lips of yours and repeat after me: "No. I'd love to help on this committee, but as the only parent I am careful to order my time for the sake of peaceful and productive routine." If you want to contribute, ask for an easy job—and do not chair a committee!

If you must contribute cookies (what mom doesn't?), you have several options:

- Make them yourself with the kids.
- Ask the kids to make them.
- Ask your mother to make them.
- Defrost a batch you made for moments like this.
- Make them with a boxed mix.
- Slice and bake.
- Buy them.

Let Your Children Help

One of the big aspects of parenting is teaching children the responsibility they need to step into adulthood with confidence and skill. I feel we undervalue the contribution our children make in day-to-day affairs. We should expect children to play a part in home life. For sure, doing things ourselves is much easier than coping with the whining, the obstinacy, or the inefficiency of children—not to mention how long it takes little fingers to learn how to tie a shoe, hold a broom, or fold a shirt. In the beginning, the ethic, not the result, is what matters.

As our standards change, children do not have much opportunity to develop skills that will help them to stand on their own feet. Parents are often so busy they never think of delegating some responsibilities to the children—age appropriate, of course. Author Eleanor Berman has commented on this phenomenon, and you may be surprised by her conclusion: "A child who could excel in sports, at schoolwork, or in social contacts was a visible symbol of parental success...Whether the children contributed their share at home mattered much less than whether they shone outside."[1]

Time-Saving Tips:

- If you work, schedule appointments to see the barber, doctor, and dentist on Saturdays. Always shoot for the first appointment of the morning so you do not have to wait.

- Create a "task co-op" with other single mothers.

- Whenever you use up something or are nearing the end of your supply (such as toilet paper, pet food, or diapers), put that item on a list on the fridge. More clasp magnets! Have two lists: "get at once" and "can wait." (If it can wait, try going without and improvising.)

- Make sure everything in your life—keys, sunglasses, and books; spices, Tupperware, and the ketchup bottle; toothpaste, aspirin, and the thermometer—has its very own "parking place" in your home, and park it there after you use it. If you learn this one thing, you will save significant time each day.

- If you have small children and you want to get things accomplished, invest in a sturdy and safe playpen. Equip it with a few of the children's toys and place it near where you are working so you are within eyesight. A playpen is not a cage; it is a sensible tool when used properly. Use it when you need two free hands. Your child will learn to entertain himself or herself.

- Store only like things in stacks, such as washcloths, towels, underwear, and storage containers. I prefer to roll things when I store them. For instance, get yourself a sturdy tub into which you put rolled tablecloths, standing on end. It may not be the prettiest method, but you can see all tablecloths at once and merely pull the one you want rather than dig under heaps of tablecloths, which will end up in a big tablecloth mess.

- Do not depend on your memory. If possible, write things down. Keep your notes in a specific place: a colorful bowl, on a cork board, near the telephone.

- Every time you look up a phone number, highlight it with a yellow highlighter.

- Invest in a feather duster and learn how to use it.

READING

Dawn E. Reno, *The Unofficial Guide to Managing Time* (Foster City, CA: IDG Books Worldwide, 2000).

Georgene Lockwood, *The Complete Idiot's Guide to Organizing Your Life* (Indianapolis: Alpha Books, 1999).

Vicki Norris, *Restoring Order* (Eugene, OR: Harvest House Publishers, 2006).

Six

Affording It All

"I still get angry about the divorce when the other parent acts like a parent only when it is convenient for him. He's moved on and moved in with another woman and had another child with her, but he hasn't paid court-ordered child support in over a year. The Attorney General's office gives a slap on the wrist and asks for promises he won't keep to pay back child support."

Shane

Before we jump headlong into financial management, I want to spend some time on your status as a single mom, especially if this situation is new to you through either death or divorce.[1] The first few years in this new role may be the hardest as you learn to stand on only two feet and possibly adjust to a different standard of living.

When Your Husband Dies

I encourage you to enlist the aid of professionals. Look for seasoned professionals who deal with estates and probate. You may need the help of an accountant, a lawyer, a banker, an insurance agent, an appraiser, and an investment counselor. If yours is a small estate with no clouds or complications hanging over it, the family lawyer may be just fine. If you are dealing with an estate of appreciable size, or if you're facing the slightest possibility of complication (claims by other heirs and so on), this is a time to get expert help.

Sit down with every single important paper you can find. If your husband had drawers and files filled with papers, methodically go through one drawer each day. Put headings on paper: investment, insurance (life and health), associations and organizations, bank accounts, legal papers, bills, real estate, military, other. Soon after your husband's death is not the time to throw anything away!

Your husband probably had some kind of insurance. Call his agent. Also check with his parents. Some parents bought insurance on children long ago that still might be in effect. Check with every single organization (even credit card companies) to see whether he has a death benefit, particularly if he died accidentally.

When Your Husband Leaves You on Your Own

If reconciliation is not possible, the marriage is dissolved, and safeguards should be in place for both parties and the children. The burden to deal justly is great in a divorce. Communication, which is usually strained and difficult, is most important. I've walked in your shoes. It is not a good time. Here are some things that can help:

- Establish your own savings and credit.
- Make an inventory of all tangible and intangible assets.
- Make certain you have adequate life insurance.
- Hire an attorney. Find a divorce lawyer and shop price. If you

are responsible for the fee in whole or in part, ask for a written statement that puts a cap on the fee.

- Check with your attorney first, but you may want to close joint charge accounts or notify businesses that you or your ex will be removed from the account.

- Check with your attorney first, but you may want to freeze all bank and investment accounts or give instructions that no transaction may take place without written approval of both parties.

- Keep cool but stand your ground. The more hostility and bickering, the higher the cost of the divorce. Ask yourself, *How will this settlement affect me when I am 65?*

- Consult an attorney to rewrite your will. Can the father attach your estate? Does child custody automatically revert to him?

- Extremely important: Ask your lawyer about establishing power of attorney with someone trustworthy who can make decisions should you become disabled and not be able to make medical decisions on your behalf or on behalf of your children. Keep the person's name in your wallet. (There is no sense establishing this if emergency and hospital personnel are unaware of the arrangement.)

- Get to know the divorce laws of your state.

What Is at Stake?

Though your marriage may be in shambles, you still need to exhibit grace and Christian behavior as you deal with such issues as custody of children, child support, alimony, and division of property. (Christian behavior, however, *does not* include staying put if you or your children are being battered!)

Custody of Children and Child Support

Custody issues can be highly charged, so consult an attorney to protect the children's interest. Do you need to consider joint custody, visitation rights, or restraining orders? Who will pay for travel if the children have to visit a parent in a faraway town? Until what age will the children be supported? Will your husband assist in extracurricular expenses, trips, medical care outside of standard insurance coverage, and college education? Who will pay for health insurance for the children? Who will benefit from tax deductions?

One of the mothers I interviewed for this book reported that court-ordered child support did not come regularly. When I questioned her about this she said she never asked her ex to pay what she felt he knew was his responsibility. I do not recommend this behavior. We should remain sensitive to the plight of men during a divorce, but human nature is predictable. If you don't report noncompliance, noncompliance is what you will reap.

Because of noncompliance of child support, most states are cracking down on deadbeat dads and have established child support administration agencies. Congress passed the Family Support Act of 1988, which enforces child support orders. Check with your state to determine if unemployment compensation can be attached for child support. Do not wait until support payments are astronomical before you file a complaint. The dad may be less likely to pay a large sum, and a settlement might forgive part of what he owes. If you are having difficulty obtaining child support, contact the helpful agencies that I've listed at the end of this chapter.

Please, please, please...the courts are not in existence to help you to get even with your ex or to punish him. Courts are good for establishing a just agreement. As bitter as you may be, for the sake of the children, please take the high road and do not let rancor enter this issue. Experts all agree that relations with your ex—especially in financial matters—should be treated as business transactions. This is a mighty tall order since this is a man with whom you've been intimate and vulnerable and with whom you have likely dreamed of growing old. Now it's come to this. And some author is telling you to act like you're going to a meeting? Yes. I'm also going to tell you to walk in the father's shoes—regardless of the reason for your divorce.

As I mentioned earlier, I have heard the other side of the story. I have heard men speak in frustration, anger, and pain that they were paying dearly to keep their children and their children's mother in relative comfort while they not only struggled financially but had to settle for visitation by permission only, pictures of their kids instead of the real thing, or no contact at all.

Asking for More Child Support

You may have valid reasons for requesting an increase in child support payments, including inflation, unexpected needs such as chronic medical or emotional problems, or the horrendous spike in car insurance when they start to drive.

As we've just learned, the father may be maxed or feeling particularly testy because he gets little in return for his contribution to his children. If the father has remarried, he may have the added pressure of resistance from his new wife, who is also trying to cope and make ends meet. And round and round it goes...

Approach the court with paperwork and figures in hand. Show that you too have contributed to any added cost, and continue to treat this issue as a business transaction. I know this sounds awful considering that you are negotiating about the care of your children, but this is the way to keep things cool. A lawyer might handle this for you.

Alimony

When I faced divorce, I was frozen with fear about money. Where would it come from? How would I survive? What should I demand? Could I demand anything? Help!

Since the advent of no-fault divorce, much of the focus has switched from alimony to custody rights and distribution of assets.

Alimony seems to be going the way of the Model T, yet some divorces still include alimony settlements. Alimony will stop once you remarry. Alimony is taxable because it is considered income rather than a distribution or settlement of property. Many women are offered a lump-sum settlement, either in cash or in real or personal property.

Existing Debt

A crucial factor in a divorce settlement is who will bear responsibility for existing debt. Your creditors do not care one whit how your separation or divorce agreement divides responsibility for debt. You are each liable for the full amount of debt on joint credit cards until the bill is paid.

Keep in mind that if the charge accounts you used with your husband were contracted jointly, you will both have the same credit history. Before you sign the final decree, make sure that all joint accounts are paid off and closed, and start new accounts in your individual names. Be careful not to run up charge account debt as retaliation. If your ex can prove that you did, you may end up footing the bill yourself.

Important Considerations

- Children are best served if they stay in their own home. Who continues the mortgage payment? If the mortgage is retired, who pays for taxes, insurance, and upkeep?

- Can you remain the beneficiary on his life insurance policy? You may request that you be named an irrevocable beneficiary, which means you cannot be removed as beneficiary without your written permission. You will also be notified if the policy is in danger of lapse.

- Will his health insurance policy cover the kids? Can your coverage continue for a while, or will he pay for you to obtain your own coverage?

- Can you claim one or two kids as dependents even though he wants to claim the children for income tax purposes? Consult a tax expert, but the IRS will usually honor a written agreement between parties about claiming dependents, regardless of primary support.

- Who will pay the attorney fees? If he doesn't pay your attorney fee (but said he would) are you then liable?

Managing Finances

Jan struck me as an informed and successful woman. She listened attentively to a talk I was giving and then followed me to the parking lot. There she leaned against her car and wept heavy tears. Jan, a single parent due to divorce, was seconds away from losing her house and car, her children were taxing her paycheck beyond belief, she was about to be delinquent with her credit card bill (which was maxed), and nobody, not even her closest friends or family, had a clue. Jan is a certified public accountant.

Many women like Jan offer pretense and bluff while staggering under crushing debt and fear. Some women's spending is out of control. They hope for temporary release from anxiety or despair—shopping as therapy, shopping as addiction. Other women struggle to live within their means and don their Wonder Woman cape daily, determined to create a happy haven for their children. Still other women choose to remain ignorant of the state of their affairs as if denial will make reality go away. Almost all manage to hide their fears and insecurities behind Sunday smiles.

Finding Your Way

- Do you have any idea how much you now owe creditors?
- If you have a mortgage, when will it be paid?

- What is the deductible on your car insurance?
- How much do you earn each year?
- Where do you find the best buys in a store?
- What are the interest rates on your credit cards?
- How much life insurance do you have? Where is the policy?
- Can you put your hands on $3000 for an emergency by tomorrow afternoon?
- Are you better off investing in a mutual fund, in stocks, or in bonds?
- When was the last time you balanced your checkbook?

If you had trouble answering the questions above, don't be overwhelmed. Whether your fear about money is tiny or as big as the sky, you'll never face anything you can't handle through God's providence. He might not send the sweepstakes squad to your door, but He will send His grace. If you are determined to become a financially secure single mother, roll up your sleeves—we've got work to do.

As we plunge deeper into this chapter, I'd like you to do a little soul-searching about your financial security. Think for a minute and jot down your thoughts:

Where am I now?_____

_____

Where would I like to be?_____

_____

Whatever your financial concern or predicament is, you will never be able to establish a strategy toward any goal unless you first know where you are. You can overcome destructive habits only when you know exactly what got you into a mess in the first place.

Debt and Denial

You may be scared witless to face your financial predicament. (One of the surest ways to do a swan dive smack into the never-ending pit of debt is to refuse to open your mail.) It's called denial. By hiding from the truth, we don't have to face the failure, the pain, or the raw terror of the mess we are in. We sink deeper and deeper into despair, denying the reality of the situation as if not facing the problem will make it go away.

Perhaps you live for the moment. (When I talk elsewhere in this book about living today, I am not recommending a cavalier nonchalance toward the future.) Perhaps you spend freely, certain your ship will dock soon and take care of all your woes. You don't plan, and you certainly don't plan on something coming along that might sink your ship. Many women deny the urgency of money management or wise spending choices and bet things will always be better by tomorrow. Or by next month. Or by this time next year.

Looking your situation in the eye and facing the music requires gumption and strength of character. If you are in financial trouble, you must take action now. The journey of a thousand miles, said a Chinese philosopher, begins with the first step.

Open your mail.[2]

This one giant step will make all the next steps on your path to financial security much easier. For now, this little exercise in terror serves one purpose alone: to force you to put long-term and short-term debt on paper and have a good long look. Once you assess your financial situation, you can find ways to improve it or to seek the help you need. We will look closely at monthly bills and living expenses a bit later. Perhaps, because of your discipline and wise planning, you will be able to fill in the following chart with ease.

	Amount of Debt	Monthly Payment	Interest Rate	Payments Remaining
Mortgage				
Auto Loan				
Short-Term Loan				
Credit Card:				
Credit Card:				
Credit Card:				
Credit Card:				
Other Debt:				
Other Debt:				
Other Debt:				
Other Debt:				
Total				

Bravo for you—just for getting through this chart! Take heart if you are frightened by the amount of debt you have amassed. Once you apply sound money management principles, you will move further away from debt and closer to financial security. The hardest part of financial management is over. The next thing you have to do is establish financial objectives by writing a mission statement.

Look at it this way: If you were in business, you would create a mission statement that clearly defined your objective in business and exactly how you were going to go about business. Call yourself "Single Mom, Ltd." and write your mission statement or objective. Make your objective short, concise, and from the heart. Here are some examples:

- I want to be out of debt in_____years.
- My children and I will learn to be content with a simpler, less consumptive lifestyle.
- The mortgage will be paid in full by_____.

- I will get the kids through college without student loans.
- I will go barging through France when I am empty-nested.
- I will become a better steward of money and possessions.

What is your objective? _____

Take Down Those Barriers!

Now consider everything that might derail you. You need to understand why you are in debt if you are having trouble financially. And then you need to know how you are going to change the situation. Consider these examples:

- The lure of easy credit is so tempting that I make purchases when I shouldn't.
- At times I could have certainly gotten along with less but didn't.
- At times I could have gone without rather than using my charge card.
- I just had to have that new car—the old one wasn't worth the cost of repairing it.

Why do you have trouble managing money? _____
_____

Now, choose some ways to manage finances better. Here are some options:

- I will cut up all but one credit card.
- I will discipline myself to use my one card wisely and use cash as much as possible.
- I will develop a payment plan and stick to it as best I can.
- I will learn to be content with little, or less, and become creative with what I have.

- I will do all this through the guidance and help of God the Holy Spirit.
- I will not become a tightfisted grump but a smart steward. I will do this by learning everything I can about money management and consumer spending.

How will you manage finances better? _____
_____

Okay—So Do It!

Now you need an action statement. Daily, weekly, or monthly lists or action plans will help you keep a good perspective. Try ideas like these:

- Rather than talk long-distance, I will write a letter today, use e-mail, or use my cell phone during unlimited-use hours.
- This week, I cut in half my impulse buying, eating out, and unnecessary shopping.
- This month, I will see what I can save by increasing insurance deductibles.
- I will explore the possibility of refinancing the house.
- I will become a "utilities detective" (more later in this chapter) and determine where and how I can save money on electricity, gas (including gasoline for the car), oil, phone, garbage, and water bills.

Write your action statement: _____
_____

To Budget or Not to Budge, There Is No Question

The final aspect to all this planning is to establish an ironclad accountability factor. You need to review your progress. Here is where an outsider will be invaluable. I do not believe we can magically transform ourselves overnight. Changing ingrained habits or poor skills takes time and effort, not to mention a lot of skinned knees. You need the help of someone you can report to someone who will remain steadfast, who will review your progress with you and give you encouragement. This person should help you set up a budget.

A budget is like meatloaf. Meatloaf requires certain ingredients; what you add to the basics depends on your recipe. Every cook has a concoction unique to her.

Budgets are like that. You have certain fixed expenses that must be paid. And then you have extra expenses, making your budget unique to you. In your budget, you set limits and prioritize. A budget shows in advance how much you plan to spend.

The word "budget" has gained a bum reputation...sort of like "diet." Why? Because most of us wake one fine morning, enthusiastically declare we are on a budget, and blow it by noon. We often fail because we don't have the skills to accomplish what we are doing. We also fail because we feel deserving. My son, who grew into a fine sociologist, said it well: "A sense of sound stewardship has been replaced by a feeling of entitlement."

For the single mother I am not talking about going out and buying expensive shoes or treating herself to a day at the spa. Entitlement for her equates to a $20 trip through the fast-food joint because she is so overwhelmed she is "entitled" to this splurge. It means justifying the expensive makeup from the shopping channel because, after all, she spends next to nothing on herself anyway. It means buying iPods for the kids because she felt sorry for them.

I want to take the threat out of budgeting because budgets are liberating, not oppressive. For instance, having a budget means knowing you only have $33.28 to spend on groceries and taking that amount in cash to the store, leaving your credit card, debit card, and checkbook at home. Learn to do that and you will become creative and resourceful in spending that $33.28 and using the groceries when you get home. Apply that concept to all your discretionary spending.

Behavior Plus Balance Equals Blessing

If you are saying, "B...b...but..." to a budget right now, think back to the meatloaf. Meatloaf is bland without salt. If a little salt is good, a whole lot is better, right? No, too much salt spoils the recipe. You've learned balance in cooking; learn it in money management. Too much freedom or too much rigidity spoils the budget process, and you lose heart.

Approach any budget plans with balance in perspectives, goals, and achievements. Allow for a little living. Always be prepared to pick yourself up, dust yourself off, and start over. Try to plan in advance how much you will spend on whim, fancy, or necessity. Work to change "b...b...but" into b...b...blessing.

Behavior plus balance equals blessing. If you are obedient to the clear commands from Scripture to faithfully manage your money (and possessions and gifts and time), you will find peace and prosperity, even in the poorest circumstance. We should be disciplined in all areas of financial management. How we own, buy, spend, and save demonstrates our understanding of Scripture and our obedience to its precepts.

How Earnest Are You?

If you earnestly want to embark on your own budget mission, the following chart may help you. It lists several spending categories, representing weekly, monthly, quarterly, or yearly financial obligations. You may use this information to create a system unique to your circumstance. Please consider keeping "Uh-oh!" and "Yay!"— incentive or affirmation that might help you stretch your dollars a wee bit more. Here's a sample:

	Week 1	Week 2	Week 3	Week 4	Total	Budget	Comments
Tithe	$50	$50	$50	$50	$200	$200	Yay!
Savings	0	$50	0	$50	$100	$200	Uh-oh!
Phone				$103	$103	$50	Yikes!
Food	$79	$43	$81	$11	$214	$200	Uh-oh!
Gas	$14	$12	$17	$14	$57	$50	Uh-oh!

Now, use these headings to create your own budget:

Giving
    tithe, pledges, charitable gifts   _____
Savings   _____
Housing
    principal, interest, insurance, taxes (or rent) _____
    maintenance and repairs   _____
    utilities (gas, electricity, water, garbage) _____
    furniture and housewares   _____
Transportation
    car payments   _____
    gas   _____
    maintenance and repairs   _____
    licenses and registrations   _____
    auto insurance   _____
Groceries and restaurants   _____
Child care   _____
Clothing, laundry, and dry cleaning   _____
Medical and dental
    insurance premiums   _____
    co-pays for appointments and medications _____
    over-the-counter medications   _____
    long-term care   _____
Life insurance   _____

Loan and debt reduction payments _____
Education _____
Telephone and cell phone _____
Internet provider and cable _____
Pet care _____
Recreation, entertainment, and vacation _____
Allowances _____
Gifts _____
Magazine subscriptions and books _____
Annual dues _____
Personal items _____
Other _____
Total _____

How can you specifically change your "uh-oh" into "yay"?_____

_____

What can you do today to limit spending? _____

_____

It Should Be Called Debit: The Very Big Business of Credit

In my opinion, the credit card industry has a death grip on us like a pit bull on a rag doll, and credit card accounts are designed to keep us in debt. Credit card companies want your soul, and they will not rest until they get their plastic in your pocket. They promise rewards, cake-and-eat-it-too living, and "everything else" lifestyle. These promises have a dark underbelly.

Depending upon whose statistic you read or which expert you listen to, the average American household is in consumer debt from $6,000 to $20,000. For some, the figure is staggeringly higher. You may be divorced as a direct result of misuse of credit cards.

When it comes to credit card debt, are you culpable? Certainly. You did not exercise restraint and got yourself into a mess...the mess of interest and assorted nasty penalty surprises that reared their heads the first time your payment was late. (Late with one credit card company might mean late fees and automatically higher interest rates on all of your credit cards.) No, you didn't get into a credit card trap by waltzing into Saks to buy a Gucci bag. You needed a diaper bag and diapers and a new transmission for the clunker and milk…and then you made a vow to catch up and not use that card again (tomorrow). Though our dependence on credit sustains a wicked system, it is the only system we have. Credit makes the world go around. If everyone cut their credit cards in half and went back to only cash, a couple things would happen: The economy would tank, and few of us would be able to function. Credit cards are nearly impossible to avoid using. Think about gas for your car. The gas pump not only takes your card on the spot but even talks to you and charms you into thinking you need to go inside the mini-mart and buy a taco. Think of self-serve checkout systems in many groceries and big-box stores. Use your credit card for convenience! Go more deeply into debt! Yahoo…and that pit bull keeps shaking its head with you clenched in its teeth and with no rescue in sight. If I sound angry, I am. I'm angry for you and millions like you who have found themselves with debt that they may never be able to repay.

What You Need to Know About Credit

Credit is a loan. It is borrowing money you will have to pay back (with interest) from future earnings. Most people take advantage of credit to buy stuff. Credit itself, like money, TV, and consumption, is not a bad thing. Credit abuse is what gets us into trouble.

Our society operates on the certainty of credit, and the power of plastic enables you to negotiate business with many vendors. Many argue that credit is a positive influence in the following ways:

Credit improves people's standard of living. It may, if you are brilliant at managing payments and factoring all the costs of credit. Credit makes just about every want immediately attainable. This may sound desirable, but for many this has been the cause of diminishing rather than improving their standard of living as credit card debt creates despair and stress. But, hey—immediate gratification! Isn't that one of the virtues we want to teach our kids?

Credit enables the consumer to take advantage of a good deal or sale. True. So you buy something on sale...say, 20 percent off. Your existing credit card has a 19 percent interest rate (it may have been low and attractive once, but your rate increased exponentially after a couple of late payments), and since you have an existing balance, the interest on new purchases begins immediately. Let's do some math. If you paid your credit card bill in full (which you did not), you "saved" 1 percent on merchandise you were quite content to be without until you fell prey to the lure of the outlet mall. Since you didn't pay your bill in full, the 1 percent savings is long gone, absorbed by the choke hold of your credit card interest. Some sale.

Credit allows you to purchase big-ticket items. This may or may not be a valid argument. Let's look at the big-ticket items in most homes. Appliances are certainly big-ticket items. Some appliance stores offer special deals for installment purchase—so many days the same as cash, no interest for the first year. (Caution! This can be a tricky deal!) If you've shopped for an item, a refrigerator for example, and the price is consistent with fair market value, it may be worth paying a little interest to enjoy the benefit of refrigeration now. Certainly, credit can sometimes work for you if you use it wisely. (Milk sours awfully fast at room temperature.)

On the other hand, resorting to interest and installments just because you got bored with your avocado fridge might be a misuse of credit. (Rumor has it avocado is coming back in style.)

Credit makes purchases more convenient. No question, some things are easier to purchase when you use credit: catalog goods, motels, and rental cars, to name a few. Using a credit card is quicker than writing a check and then producing a driver's license (and often two credit cards) to validate it.

But what difference does it make if you take 30 more seconds to write a check? If you are in such a big hurry, pay with cash. Or use a debit card. Debit cards have all the appearance of credit cards with one big difference: When the plastic card is run through the store's computer, the cost of your purchase is automatically deducted from your bank account.

Credit enables us to better manage finances. Yes, some people are efficient and systematic, and they pay everything in full or on time. So having the credit card bill simplifies matters. This point is valid only in those cases when individuals keep track of their spending and pay off their credit card balance each month.

Credit helps us to establish a favorable credit rating. Absolutely, positively, yes—unless you miss a few payments. If you are the kind of person who pays off the balance on your credit card each month, credit cards may be a way for you to get credit. Creditors put your income and your bill-paying history under a microscope when you apply for a loan. Unless you are certain you will never apply for a mortgage, or any kind of loan ever, or rent an apartment, or apply for a job, you need good credit history.

Credit helps us to cope with financial emergencies. True. More than one person has suddenly had to take a flight because of a medical or family emergency. At a time of stress, the convenience of credit is handy. Your best bet, though, is to have an emergency fund for such occurrences.

A good emergency fund is equal to at least three months' salary. On hand. Untouched. Emergency only. A family trip to Disneyland is not an emergency regardless of how hard you try to justify it. You're much more entitled to sleep well at night because your bills are paid and you're ready for a rainy day. Get that emergency fund in place. Then save and go to Disneyland.

Credit helps us to keep savings intact. Yes and no. Once again, this depends on your overall ability to manage money. If your savings are collecting a higher interest through some investment, for instance, and you'd face interest penalties for withdrawing before maturity, it might be better to go with a small loan. Credit cards rarely qualify as a substitute unless they carry a low interest rate. And, oh boy, read the fine print on your credit card agreement to learn about costs associated with cash advances.

It's Not Your Money

Mark this down: When you use a credit card or borrow funds, you are not spending your money, you are spending someone else's! Here are some hard, cold facts about credit:

- Credit is a loan. It is your future income already spent. Kaput.
- Credit provides false security. Plastic in your hand gives you a feeling of power and control.
- Every single study proves that we spend more when we use a credit card or a debit card.
- Conservative statistics tell us that many Americans are up to their limit on credit. Twenty percent or more of their monthly income goes to debt reduction.
- Credit holds hidden costs. Finance charges and interest add substantially to the cost of your purchase, as do late payment (and with some companies, early payment!) penalties.
- Abuse of credit can destroy your creditworthiness and actually lead to loss of what you already have. Just ask Sarah. Her story is extreme, but true.

Sarah was in a heap of trouble. On her own with two children after her husband, John, walked out, she amassed crippling debt on her credit cards. Instead of asking for help, she kept her financial problems to herself.

At first, Sarah's teaching salary, combined with child support, was adequate. The child support paid the mortgage. But eventually she needed it for credit installments, and ultimately (because she was totally out of control) Sarah simply spent the money recklessly.

Sarah's debt began to mount as she started using her charge card for everything including her groceries and her gas. She felt sorry for her kids, so she outfitted them with new wardrobes. In a few months, the collectors started to call. She left incoming phone calls to the answering machine and hid any mail that looked like a bill (or a threat) in a box in the basement. She even tried to hide from the sheriff when he came to deliver her foreclosure notice. She hadn't paid her mortgage in months.

Sarah was utterly despondent. The paralysis of her fear kept her from facing her spending problems and dealing with them. In the end she lost everything. John was awarded temporary custody of the children until she demonstrated she had stopped her destructive spending behavior.

Though Sarah's story is an extreme case, financial counselors nod their heads in sad confirmation and tell me that unless many other people change their destructive spending behavior, they will follow in her footprints. Sarah is now in counseling and working hard to overcome her addiction to spending. For her—and for many people—easy credit is far too easy to abuse.

You may not have a compulsive need to spend, and you may be responsible enough to handle credit. If so, for you, the good aspects of credit may outweigh the negatives.

Credit Card Savvy

The responsible use of a credit card is utterly necessary. Here are a few tips to help you to manage your card responsibly.

- Get out your magnifying glass and read the fine print of your credit contract. Make certain you understand what its says. If you don't understand, call and ask, ask, ask until you are fully satisfied that you do understand the terms of your credit.

- You should not be paying an annual fee for a credit card.

- Look for the lowest interest you can find.

- Watch out for two-cycle billing or language on your card that says something like "including new purchases." This means if you are carrying a balance, the credit card company can charge retroactive interest. You definitely want a card that excludes new purchases if you ever carry a balance.

- Determine if you are paying extra fees: transaction fees, finance charges on top of interest, excessive fees for exceeding your credit limit, paying late, or (get this) paying your balance in full each month.

- Make certain you understand how long your grace period is to pay your bill before interest is added on. Some companies are shortening grace periods, making it pretty hard to avoid interest charges. I heartily recommend that you pay all bills when you receive them.

FICO: Your Credit Score

A FICO score is a credit rating developed by the Fair Isaac Corporation. You need to know your credit score—it's the number that lenders look at when you ask for credit. Scores run from 300 to 850, and a good score is considered anything over 700. Go below 600 and you may end up with higher interest rates...or be denied credit.

What is your FICO based on? Your bill-paying history and how much you owe. Nothing else comes into the score, not your income or marital status, education, or the job you hold. An important thing to know about your credit score is that even though the score reflects you and your payment history, joint debt can affect your individual score.

By now you've no doubt heard that it is prudent to obtain a copy of your credit report from the three major credit bureaus (Equifax,

TransUnion LLC, and Experion). Learning your score, and improving it if it is low, is just as important. A brochure on FICO can help you do just that. You can obtain "Your Credit Scores Publication" online at www.pueblo.gsa.gov or by calling 888-878-3256. Also check out www.myfico.com.

What Are You Teaching Your Children?

The Bible tells us in Proverbs 22:6 to "train a child in the way he should go, and when he is old he will not turn from it." You are responsible to teach your child thrift and sound money management. How do you do that? By example.

Let me ask you this: How many times do the kids see you whip out your credit card? Do the kids hear arguments about money? Do the kids have a way of talking you into everything they want? What on earth are you teaching them?

Children are costly. Demands on the pocketbook are relentless. From care to feeding to education to clothes, kids are an expensive proposition. I'd like to address the specific issue of the needs, wants, and desires of that insatiable little consumer of yours. Here are some suggestions.

Mute the TV commercials. The constant onslaught of commercials is downright criminal. If you, an adult, can be seduced into buying a product because of its dramatic claims and punchy jingle, think how a child's mind is affected. This is worrisome.

Set limits when your kids are in the cradle. You will naturally want to buy every cute baby outfit and gadget the stores have to offer. Cool it. For one thing, children grow too fast. For another, they need sturdy, long-wearing clothes rather than a closet full of frills. You are the one getting the thrill from your child looking like a model. Give your children messages right from the beginning; teach them a simple, godly life. That is abundance enough.

Talk to your children in their language as soon as they can comprehend.

"We don't do that" or "No way, Jose" just won't do. Kids live in a social world and are pressured to fit in. Peer pressure is a big issue for children, especially adolescents and teens. Simply crossing your arms and slamming your foot down might create hurt and rebellion.

Define financial parameters to the children. Assemble bills and notepad and convene a family meeting when no one is hurried. The purpose of the meeting is to show the kids your income and outgo. Use dollar bills and coins—or beans—to illustrate. Do not ever insinuate that your children's security is threatened or that they are responsible to share the burden of financial care.

Ask them what they think they could do to cut back or to save. Be sure to provide incentive for success, such as a recreation or vacation jar to collect savings.

One more thing: Don't deny your kids everything. Nothing is wrong with treating your children to something they wish for once in a while. What you can't give your child in material things you can make up for with creativity and joy that comes from your mother's heart.

Allowances

I believe in an allowance. The amount of allowance should be within reason for both you and the child, and allowances should have strings attached.

Decide whether you are paying your children for chores they perform at home. I did not believe Josh should be paid for doing his fair share, but I did offer him a bonus when he did something extra.

I'd recommend a written contract that outlines exactly what items the child is fiscally responsible for. These might include such things as movies, movie rentals, snacks, school lunch, or personal items such as school supplies, clothes, savings, and gifts.

Sanyika Calloway Boyce, a financial coach and author, suggests making an older child responsible for a cell phone bill, stating that cell phone companies don't fool around: no pay, no coverage. "They don't have any sympathy," Calloway Boyce says. "Kids need to learn that."[3]

Retirement

Having written a book called *Living Well in Retirement*, I am aware of the complex issues facing women when they grow older. Though the purpose of this book is to help you to live well now, I would be remiss not to urge you to establish a retirement plan. You may be planning for retirement by not having a plan: planning to stay healthy and strong so you can work until the day you die, planning to be dependent on your grown children, planning to live in near-poverty conditions, planning to face years of anxiety and anguish over bills. Some plan, huh? Listen to Martha, who heads a bank near my town:

"The smartest thing a woman can do to protect herself financially is to start saving for retirement. You can't start too soon, and it's only going to get more expensive to maintain your lifestyle."

Increasing the Means You Live Within

Work is a big factor for the single mom. Lots of mothers maintain full-time jobs they do not like just because of benefits: health insurance, vacations, retirement, and the security of knowing a paycheck will come week after week. Yet a full-time job makes parenting (solo or not) a real challenge.

Part-time work would be the ticket for lots of moms if they didn't sacrifice those benefits. It is a real conundrum. For sure, working flex hours (or working for yourself) has benefits for the single mom. If you feel this is something you need to do, think about your education, your experience, your training, and your natural skills to determine which direction you might go to find (or make) work. Let me get some brainstorming started:

- If you're a stay-at-home mom, you might provide child care for other children. Check the laws of your state, county, and city to see how many children you can care for without being considered a day care facility, which would require licensing, bonding, health inspection, insurance, and more. If you do consider babysitting an option, be sure to check with your insurance carrier to confirm that you have liability coverage should something happen to a child in your care. And of course you would want to take every precaution to protect any children you care for.

- A young single mom I know lives in the country and has a dog and cat boarding service. Anything to do with pets, from doggy day care to pet walking to grooming to photography might be worth considering if you have the facility and the know-how. People spend a lot of money on their pets. (Again, check to be sure your insurance is adequate.)

- Many people have been successful buying and selling through on-line auctions.

- Typing, copyediting, and bookkeeping are always in demand. You may even find a demand for those with time and skill to load iPods.

- Housecleaning can bring in good money if you are efficient and trustworthy.

- Seasonal yard work and property management are good money-makers. (These may require bonding and insurance.)

Eating Within Your Means

Eat seasonally. Buying produce in season is less expensive and better for you. Eat foods within the natural rhythm of life. Savor strawberry shortcake on the Fourth of July, apple pie in the fall, and asparagus when daffodils are blooming.

Stock up on seasonal bargains and loss leaders. Baking supplies are usually slashed in price during Thanksgiving and Christmas holidays. Picnic supplies drop in price in June. Stores will offer special deals on hams at Easter, corned beef in March. Stock up when prices are attractive.

Don't waste. No sense cutting a great deal on lettuce if it rots in the fridge. Certainly, some things will get old before their time and sound the green goop alert. It happens to us all. Try to store food wisely and use it before it goes to waste. Decommission the garbage disposal—the average American household wastes one-half pound of food each day. This is appalling.

Use coupons—sometimes. No sense buying something with a coupon if it is not something you would normally buy. Try to use the coupon on a sale item for a double whammy.

Use what you have. Most of us could feed our family for weeks by using what we've amassed in the cupboards and freezer.

Buy in bulk. Any time you pay a store to package or process something for you, you pay more. Sometimes, however, convenience is worth its weight in shredded mozzarella.

A Few Food Shopping Tips

- Go to the grocery store as seldom as possible. (Ditto all other stores.)

- Shop with a list and stick to it. Leave two spaces blank for loss leaders or an occasional impulse item.

- Buy only what you eat and eat what you buy.

- Don't shop when you are hungry—you will buy more.

- Leave the kids at home. Shop alone—you will purchase more when you are with another person.

- Eye-level products are often more expensive. Better for you to bend and reach anyway.

- Many stores will break up bunches of produce to sell you a smaller amount. This is a good way to buy celery. Ask.

- Buy spices and herbs in bulk from the health food store or bulk food store. Buy small quantities because spices lose their strength over time. For helpful instructions on how to shop a health food store, see *Ditch the Diet and the Budget.*

- If you buy cereal, try to stay clear of name-brand boxed cereals. Buy generic or make oatmeal. The cereal aisle is one of the most expensive in the grocery store. And one of the least healthy.

- Buy generic or store brands unless you are loyal to a particular product.
- Read labels. Remember that ingredients are listed by weight.
- Do not always grab the special on the end of the aisle. Many times a similar product in the middle of the aisle is less expensive.
- Buy favorite foods (and foods that will be used) in the largest volume possible.
- Know your prices and shop the sales. If you do better at a warehouse store, shop there. Buy as much as you need for the foreseeable future and always be prepared for possible emergency or natural disaster.
- Try not to examine something unless you really intend to purchase the product. If you pick up a product, you have a 50 percent chance of buying it.
- Never buy a dairy product without checking the expiration date.
- Watch the register when your sales are rung up. Scanners and people make mistakes. Checkers commonly run an item through the scanner twice.
- Start a group. Share money-saving tips with each other, boost each other through hard times, and give each other accountability. Use your purchasing power to buy in bulk and share your purchase.

How to Make Your Grocery Dollar S-t-r-e-t-c-h

- Learn how to cook. This is not as silly a suggestion as it sounds. Invest in an easy cookbook or visit your grandma. Cooking savvy will help you stretch your food budget a long way. What is the sense of investing in an inexpensive product (cornmeal, for instance), if you don't know how to make polenta, cornbread, or tamale pie?
- Plan what you are going to cook in advance. This is not as hard as it sounds. It eliminates the impulsive "What am I going to fix for dinner?" and your panicky dash to the store.
- Prepare only as much food as you need. Do not cook so much

that some food turns into a science project in the fridge and is ultimately thrown away.

- Prepare more food than you need. Prepare enough to create an entire separate meal and freeze it. Eventually you will be taking from and adding to your freezer stash routinely. Also, try to have enough left over to serve breakfast or lunch the next day.
- Learn to eat smaller portions. Start to take notice how full your plate usually is. Eat slowly.
- Cut down on expensive desserts. Designer ice cream is fun once in a while, but a steady diet is bad for your budget and your waist!

Dressing Within Your Means

Seasonal inventory. In order to sell off inventory, stores offer clearance or out-of-stock sales at drastically reduced prices. Few stores send inventory back to a warehouse. Winter and fall clothing should begin to be cleared around the end of January. This is an excellent time to buy a great sweater for someone's upcoming birthday. Start watching for spring closeouts around the last week in April.

Stores start clearing out summer clothing in the middle of July. Many stores try to be 100 percent back-to-school by then. Certainly, by the end of summer you will find spectacular buys on lightweight clothing. Why not buy a cotton skirt to tuck away as a Christmas present? Most fall and back-to-school clothing will close out around the end of October.

Sales. The best sales are usually clearance sales, which start at 30 percent off. (Just about every piece of clothing in a store will sport a 25 percent markdown at one time or another.) "Red tag" is another thing to look for; it means the item has been marked down drastically. You may find pre-season sales as well. These usually top off at 25 percent markdowns on clothes for the upcoming season—often as much as three months before the season begins. The bonus to pre-season buying is the increased selection.

Clothes Buying Tips

- Merchandise is normally displayed 30 days before it is put on sale.

- "Clean up in season" is a sacred phrase in retail. It means items with a seasonal application must be sold during that season or holiday time. For instance, consider Valentine's Day, the most costly day for retail stores. Buying inventory for this holiday is difficult. What's a merchant to do with two dozen heart-shaped boxes of candy on February 15? Retailers reduce prices dramatically on goods that have lingered beyond the peak selling period.

- Think "timeless," not "dated." No matter where you buy clothes, opt for timeless, classic styles that will survive each new season's fashion industry assault. For example, one necessary outfit is a great-fitting pair of slacks or a skirt, crisp white blouse, and blazer.

- If you are patient, trips with your clothes shopping list to the mall (several department stores) during any of the projected out-of-stock sales will probably net you a terrific buy. This is a good time to buy presents. (You should only go to the mall when you absolutely need something.)

- Learn to accessorize and use color to your advantage.

- Always factor in your cleaning bills. Clothes that require special cleaning can eventually cost up to three times as much. Rayon and wool almost always need dry-cleaning.

- "Specials" are usually sales for items seldom or never carried before. Often "this ad only" offers, and usually loss leaders, represent a special deal the retailer got from a manufacturer. Traditionally, the quality is poorer than normal merchandise.

- Avoid high traffic areas stocked with impulse items! This merchandise has the highest markup and is usually the "in" fashion. Best sales are found in the back of the department.

- Do what I do...check the racks at Goodwill first!

How to Shop in Goodwill or in a Clothing Outlet

- Some labels are sure bets of good quality.
- Don't be afraid of a rip or tear as long as it's something you can mend. If you find a flaw, bring it to the attention of the clerk for possible reduced cost.
- Check to see if the sewing is straight and without puckers.
- High-quality buttons are a sure sign of quality.
- Try the garment on if possible.
- Always think about your color and style.

> "The word 'sale' does not mean 'shop.'"
> *Marcie*

Sporting Goods or Exercise Equipment

How do you find sporting gear for you and the kids when you are strapped for cash? Educate yourself!

- Determine the quality and type of equipment you want.
- Find out what the normal retail price would be.
- Watch your local trading paper, the classified ads, and yard sales. Check with stores that sell used sporting goods.
- Approach a coach. Ask if he knows a source for good quality used equipment in his or her particular sport.

Nine Ways to Lower Your Homeowners Insurance Costs

1. Shop around. Always ask what you can do to lower the cost. Get quotes.
2. Raise your deductible. This means you will bear the cost of all small claims.
3. Buy your home and auto insurance from the same insurer. You will

usually benefit from a lower insurance cost on both policies if they are with the same company.

4. Consider the home you buy. Know ahead of time how much insurance will cost. For instance, if you live in the forests or mountains in an area that does not have fire protection (and live in a log home with a wood-burning stove), your insurance cost is going to be mighty high, if you can even get it. New plumbing and electrical systems will many times warrant a discount. Brick construction in the east is an asset because of resistance to wind; frame construction in the west is an asset because of resistance to earthquake. Stay clear of areas that flood...homeowners insurance does not cover flood-related damage. Also, the insurance company will be interested in whether your town has a full-time or volunteer fire service, or if your house is close to a hydrant or fire station.

5. Insure your house, not the land.

6. Increase your home security. Discounts are readily available for such things as a smoke detector, a burglar alarm, or dead bolt locks. Before you buy any kind of fire or burglary protection, check with your insurance carrier to know just how much you will save in premiums.

7. Don't smoke. Smoking accounts for thousands of residential fires each year. Some companies actually reduce premiums if no family members smoke. Besides, think of the money you will save on cigarettes and chemotherapy.

8. Inspect your limits and coverage annually. Don't spend money for coverage you don't need.

9. Some people live in a high-risk area (one that may be subject to coastal storms, fires, or crime) and purchase high-risk homeowners insurance. Check with an insurance agent in the private market. You may be able to get insurance at a lower cost.

Eight Questions to Ask When Buying Health Insurance

1. Ask about coinsurance. How much of the bill do you pay?

2. Ask about your deductible. A deductible is how much money you pay out of pocket before the insurance company pays its share. Usually, the higher the deductible, the lower the premium.

3. Ask if there is a stop-loss limit. This means you only have to pay up to a certain amount and then no more. For instance, a policy may specify that after you pay $2000 out of pocket they will then pay 100 percent of medical expenses.

4. Ask about exclusions. This has to do with things your policy may not cover. Some exclusions are typical, such as outpatient mental health, cosmetic surgery, maternity, and long-term health care. Also, preexisting conditions may or may not be excluded.

5. Ask to see the insurance company's list of reasonable costs. These are the amounts the policy will reimburse you for specific medical costs, based on what the insurance company considers to be the going rate in your region. Be persistent; some companies do not like to reveal this information.

6. Ask if you can renew. Be sure the policy has guaranteed renewal. You don't want an insurer to refuse to renew if you get sick!

7. Ask about waiting periods. How long do you have to be working before coverage kicks in?

8. Ask about preapproval requirements. Insurance companies usually require advance notification for treatment plans or surgeries.

Tips on Getting Financial Aid for College[4]

1. Appeal to the financial aid office rather than trying to negotiate.

2. Exhaustively search for scholarship opportunities. Besides asking the college itself if they have scholarships, ask if they know of other sources.

3. Look into the Federal Stafford Loan for subsidized funding.

4. Consider a less expensive school, or start with two years at a local community college before transferring.

Home Energy Audit

Turn the first week of November into an energy audit week, followed by a family meeting over tacos or pizza. (Set this date as a reminder to change all batteries in smoke alarms.) Ask your local utility if a representative will visit (without charge) to help with energy-saving tips. Build your family meeting around that visit. Display utility bills and talk about your monthly payments. Prowl around the house, inside and out. Look for places where weather stripping and caulking could do some good. Check all faucets. Read your electric meter every night for a week and discover which day consumed the most energy. Figure out why. Help the kids develop math skills by determining how much electricity all of your small appliances use. Use coins to demonstrate cost or projected savings. Award a prize to the child who conserved the most energy during the week.

Energy Consumption

When cooking indoors...

- Don't preheat your oven unless a recipe calls for it.
- Turn off the oven unless a recipe calls for it.
- Use pots that fit the size of the cooktop's heating element. Keep lids on pots when cooking.
- Be sure reflector pans are clean.
- Try to bake more than one thing if you are going to heat up your oven.

Around the house...

- Keep your hot water heater at 120 degrees.
- Use shades and blinds that filter out high levels of sunlight. Keep them closed on sunny sides of your home in summer, open in winter.
- Keep your heat pump or air conditioner thermostat set on 78 or

higher. Each degree you lower it costs about 3 percent more in energy costs.

- Keep hot or cold conditioned air in the house by using exhaust fans in baths and kitchens only when absolutely necessary.

- For maximum comfort, use ceiling fans to keep cooled air circulating throughout your home.

- Keep out extra heat by turning off unneeded lights around the house or cooking meals outdoors on the grill. Take short, warm showers instead of long, hot baths.

- If you have a dishwasher, use the energy-save features and let dishes air dry. This saves time and money and keeps unnecessary heat out of the kitchen.

- If you depend on a window air-conditioning unit to keep cool, install one on the north or shaded side of the house to keep it from the sun's heat. Also, close off rooms that are not in use.

- Check the filter on your heat pump or central air-conditioning system. Cleaning or replacing filters monthly is one of the best ways to keep your unit operating efficiently.

_____ RESOURCES: CHILD SUPPORT _____

National Child Support Enforcement Association provides four major services: locating noncustodial parents, establishing paternity, establishing support orders, and collecting support payments. The program also provides services to noncustodial parents. Contact your local Health and Human Services Agency. (www.acf.hhs.gov)

Federal Parent Locator Service is the national locator system to assist states in locating noncustodial parents, putative fathers, and custodial parties for the establishment of paternity and child support obligations, as well as the enforcement and modification of orders for child support, custody, and visitation. Individuals may not make direct requests to the FPLS but can work with state or local agencies. Any request to the FPLS must go through a state parent locator service. In addition, in the event of parental kidnapping, custody, or visitation, all requests must first go through the court.

OTHER RESOURCES

"Your Credit Scores" is a helpful online article by the Consumer Federation of America. (888-878-3256, www.pueblo.gsa.gov)

The Council for Adult and Experiential Learning is a national nonprofit organization that creates and manages effective learning strategies for working adults through partnerships with employers, higher education, government, and labor. (312-499-2600, www.cael.org)

READING

Cynthia Yates, *Living Well on One Income in a Two-Income World* (Eugene, OR: Harvest House Publishers, 2003).

Cynthia Yates, *Ditch the Diet and the Budget...and Find a Better Way to Live* (Eugene, OR: Harvest House Publishers, 2004).

Cynthia Yates, *Living Well in Retirement* (Eugene, OR: Harvest House Publishers, 2005).

Robert D. Manning, *Credit Card Nation* (New York: Basic Books, 2000).

Seven

Staying Healthy Through It All

Warning: Stern language ahead.

Nothing arouses more passion in me than the state of our health and proper nutrition (aka real food). Through the past many years I have studied matters of health (in particular the effect real food has on our well-being) and have become convinced we can reap positive improvement in health, happiness, and weight issues.

So, Mom, in spite of my reassurance about not wishing to cause more work, guilt, or pressure for you...I'm doing a flip-flop of epic proportions. In this chapter my intent is to incite you to action as I zero in on only four issues: stress, movement, rest, and nutrition. All four of these issues fundamentally impact the quality of our lives and our children's lives.

Some Life

This book is about living *well*, which must include robust health and long life. Though we now statistically live longer, our lives are filled with aches, pains, drugs, disease and sickness, expensive medical treatment, unhappiness, and misery. Some life.

I read the headlines every day, and so do you: Obesity is on the rise, diabetes is skyrocketing, attention deficit disorder is projected to hit significantly more children (and adults), and Alzheimer's is predicted to rise by 35 percent in the next 20 years. And how about this one: an article titled "Health Care Tab Ready to Explode" quotes a government projection that the nation's tab for health care could hit $3.6 trillion by 2014.[1] Why are we so sick? Haven't generations been told not to smoke or do drugs, to exercise, to eat well, on and on? $3.6 trillion is a whole lot of sick.

Beyond a doubt, people have genetic predispositions to particular medical conditions, and we have all heard of such dangers as environmental toxins. Even when people are weakened by congenital defects, proper nutrition and care of the body will usually give them a better life. Teresa of Avila said, "Be friendly to your body so that the soul enjoys living in it."

You must understand, Mom, that the quality of your life and your children's lives relies totally on you getting this message. Stop with the excuses about convenience, about children's resistance, about no time, about costs, about your own lack of interest in such matters as healthy habits and nutrition. Do you want your children to grow with strong bones and teeth, healthy weight, a great self-image, vitality, a better chance to get good grades and do well in sports, and a positive outlook on life? Or do you want to consign your children to a life of obesity or failure to thrive, arthritis, poor circulation, runny noses, chronic cough and illness, lethargy, poor self-image, poor performance, and a negative outlook on life? Time for another headline: "One-Third of Kids Destined to Be Diabetic."[2]

Which of those profiles is your choice for your children? At one time, the questions I posed would have seemed odd and unnecessary. But these questions are vital to effective parenting. The health issues we face today were rare or unheard of in past generations. A fat kid was an oddity. A malnourished waif would be "fattened" by every grandmother in a 50-mile radius. A child with diabetes was pitied for the sorrow of having been so born. Attention deficit was consigned to age-related mischief or activity.

Our lack of attention to preventive care and our lack of sensible compliance to sound nutrition are damning our children's lives to poor quality and sickness. We are facing a frightening pandemic that will only worsen unless we wake up. Here are a few scenarios to drum this home.

Scenario 1: You are 41 and have not really taken care of your health. What's more, you've smoked. You have a couple of kids, and the father is out of the picture. You are getting by all right, but no great shakes. You have a debilitating stroke, and though you are very much alive, you are rather seriously disabled and dependent. Now what?

Scenario 2: Your doctor calls you into her consultation room to announce you have advanced stages of breast cancer. What does this mean to you and your children?

Scenario 3: Hard as you try, you just can't get out of bed. You can't do it. Your body is full of pain; your emotions are so low you wish you were dead. You don't even care about the kids. Doesn't anyone understand?

Scenario 4: Your kitchen cupboards are stocked with sandwich cookies, boxes of "meal makers," breakfast cereals galore, soda pop, pasta up the gazoo, chips up the gazoo, sports drink powders, cake mixes, and a few canned peas. Your child's doctor somberly tells you that your 12-year-old son has type 2 diabetes. (Sadly, your reaction is to ask what daily pill you can give him, a pill being so much simpler than ridding your cupboards of all that fun stuff and going through the hassle of changing his [and the entire family's] eating habits.)

Were those scenarios realistic? Were those scenarios preventable? You can't convince me otherwise.

Wake Up

You've got to wake up, get off the couch, get off the processed foods, and start taking care of yourself and your children in a healthier manner. No exceptions. No excuses. In order to do this you have to work to banish stress from your life. Stress is one of the biggest triggers of ill health facing us today.

> "I don't really get sick unless
> I am really stressed-out and exhausted."
>
> *Shane*

Di-stress or De-stress

Stress makes us sick and stress kills us. We all have stress in our lives, and single moms take the prize in this category. Some stress is normal; most stress is like a pack of killer bees that swarm through our systems and attack everything in sight, stinging over and over, relentlessly assaulting us from the inside out until we are too weak to withstand their onslaught. And then sickness comes, disease comes, heart attacks come. Approximately 80 percent of all visits to primary care physicians stem from stress-related issues.[3] Problems ranging from dandruff to teeth grinding have been attributed to stress. Stress is the by-product of not coping with your circumstance. Let's talk about coping once more.

Again, think about today. Do not think about tomorrow and what might happen, and do not dwell on yesterday. If you dwell on the past, says Simone Kosog, you end up a prisoner of history. She reminds us that when God saved Lot and his family, He told them not to look back, and that she who looks back "will become ossified, turned into a column of salt or an old grouch who takes no pleasure in the present, the only time we really have."[4] My friend Judy reminds me that God calls Himself I AM, not I WAS or I WILL BE. Though He transcends all time (and always was and always will be), He is the God of right now.

Stress Busters

- Get a steno pad and journal your stress away. Give your journal a name, like Nancy or Fred or Pinky Petunia, and write to Pinky with a vengeance. Put all your feelings on paper. Be sure to date your entry…it may be good for a laugh (or a cry) at a later time.

- If stress comes from another person, write him or her a letter. Let it all out, no holds barred. Then destroy the letter. Take it to a safe place outside and burn it as a stress offering to God.

- One quick, effective, and easy way to counter stress is to take a deep breath. Think about our natural response when a child is stressed and upset. What do we say? "Clench your fists and breathe rapidly?" No! We say, "Calm down and take a deep breath."

So, single mom, calm down, take a deep breath, and become resolute and excited about how you are going to positively change the quality of your family's life—with God's help—today.

Temple or Trash Dump

Your body was designed by God. We know that through sin, sickness and death entered our reality way back in the Garden of Eden. This does not take the responsibility of proper stewardship from us. The Bible is clear: We are temples of God the Holy Spirit; we are not our own. Are you treating your body like a temple or a trash dump?

Most of us want to feel good, but what we really want is to look good. We want to look the way Madison Avenue has taught us to look. Let's dispense with that thinking this very minute. Very few of us have been born with the long legs and high cheekbones of those who are in the modeling business. That's why they are models and we are not. We must accept who we are and strive for shining health.

Repeat after me: Beauty does not come from a box. Or a tube. Or an injection. Or an amazing makeover. Beauty comes from the inside and radiates out. I've known people who were so unattractive they'd make a freight train take a dirt road, yet some sort of inner glow made those people beautiful to look at and to be around. If you attain inner peace and combine it with good health, you have a guaranteed formula for outward beauty.

You want to be beautiful? Stay healthy. Health equals beauty. Health is very much a mind, body, and spirit thing, and it comes with balance and wholeness of all three. What we eat, how we live, what we do, how we act and react, and even what we believe has an impact on our health. So why don't we follow through with our plans toward better health and appearance? Because we are only skin deep.

Go Organ-ic

Do yourself a favor. Buy a children's book called *How It Works: the Human Body,* by Kate Barnes.[5] Study this book. Read in rapt wonder at the amazing complexity of your body's organs. Study the pictures to gain a better understanding of what you look like inside, under your skin.

- Turn to pages 10 to 13 and stare at the heart. Ask yourself how long a machine could work without ever stopping before it broke down. Ponder this inconceivable marvel. Think about its nonstop beating—*thumpa, thumpa, thumpa*—that sends life-giving blood to farthest extremities. What are you doing to keep your heart fit?

- Turn to pages 14 and 15 and stare at the lungs. Think about breath that gives life. Think about taking a deep breath, about God breathing life into us. Then think about the assault on our lungs from cigarette smoke and toxins in our environments. What are you doing to keep your lungs clear?

- Turn to pages 16 and 17 and stare at the skeletal structure. Look at the joints where bones come together. Think about loss of movement through such things as arthritis, about aches and pains when joints become brittle from poor nutrition or poor use. What are you doing to keep your skeletal structure strong and upright?

- Turn to pages 20 and 21 and stare at the digestive system. More importantly, stare at what the young boy is eating: one of the stars of good nutrition—an unpeeled apple. Think about intestines that have become sluggish due to lack of dietary fiber and from a deficit of good water. Take a good long look at those intestines. Think about being a storehouse for fecal waste. What are you doing to keep your intestines clean?

- Turn to pages 25 and 26 and stare at the critically important liver and kidneys. Look at them and think about their hard work when they detoxify and cleanse our systems. Think about the pancreas, which is battered with refined, processed, or high glycemic foods that cause it to produce more and more insulin until it is overtaxed, resulting in diabetes and other things. What are you doing to support these vital organs?[6]

- Now think about your children.

Give your body a fighting chance. The next time you reach for something that you know will put strain on your body, remind yourself of your deep goal to achieve health. Exercise your heart, learn to breathe correctly, stop smoking, strengthen your bones, eat unrefined foods with good fiber, get rest, and drink plenty of filtered water daily.

Movement

Let me fling another headline your way: "Why the U.S. Is Developing More Exercise Deficiency Syndrome."[7] Great. Now we give sloth a medical term.

Our serious exercise deficit is one topic on which every medical

> *"No pill I can prescribe is as effective as exercise."*
> Dr. Pamela Roberts Oehrtman

professional and nutritionist resoundly agree: Movement is health. I know moving is difficult when you are overweight, when your body hurts, or when each step is so painful you want to cry. I know motivating yourself again and again is hard. That's why I'm talking to you and not to the women who wear those nifty nylon tights, have 15 pairs of running shoes, and dangle barbells from their earlobes. I am talking to those of you who are unhealthy or overweight or miserable prisoners of history.

(In fairness to a young friend named Andy, who wears those nifty nylon tights and is a military mom, listen to how she copes: "Exercise! During the five months my husband was deployed I trained and participated in three triathlons. My schedule forced me to have time by myself, and the exercise was a fantastic outlet for me. Our local YMCA provided child care, and family and friends helped as well.")

No lecture on obesity—you've heard it all, you know it all. But if your children are overweight or obese, I'm calling you on it because this is inexcusable. Let me introduce a few statistics which I will repeat in this chapter: One in three kids born in 2001 will develop type 2 diabetes sometime during their lives; for Hispanic and African-American kids, the odds are one in two.[8]

We're all looking for magic pills, right? I know of two. They are right under our noses and they are called feet. Move them. Exercise truly does seem to be a magic pill for what ails us. (As does humor, which can be considered inner movement.) We release feel-good endorphins when we move (and when we laugh).

Things like knitting, reading, and quiet contemplation are excellent tools to calm you and to bring you into focus and serenity, but I also highly recommend a vigorous walk around the neighborhood and a good belly laugh. When you are down in the dumps, tense, and lethargic, you need these remedies the most. Go figure: At exactly the moment you want to crawl into bed and pull the covers over your head, movement will bring you a more positive outlook or greater resolve to tackle what's causing the stress; at exactly the moment you don't want to be happy, happiness will bring you better health and relief from stress.

Three important aspects of exercise are aerobics, flexibility, and weight bearing. Aerobic exercise is strenuous and gets your heart pumping. Flexibility increases range of motion and makes the body more fluid. Weight bearing strengthens bones and muscles, and it helps your body to burn fat more effectively.

Some Moving Ideas for You and Your Children

- Engage children in activities that are fun and encourage movement. If you are at work and the kids are without movement doing homework before you come home, go for a stroll after dinner.
- Dance in the living room. Turn off the TV. Ban Game Boy. Get your children to play.
- Inquire at school about extracurricular activities.
- Take up a family sport. If your finances are low, buy bikes at Goodwill, swim at the town pool, or take a hike. Every state has excellent guide books with information about hiking trails. Almost all city areas have maps of municipal nature trails.
- If at all possible (considering danger from predators or traffic), children should walk to school. This goes for you and your work too.

Rest

> "Life takes too much energy. I fall into bed in a heap."
> *Marcie*

> "If only I could sleep at night...that's when it all hits me."
> *Dottie*

You have got to get your sleep. Lack of proper sleep is implicated in a host of medical problems, including obesity. According to a

National Health and Nutrition Examination Survey conducted by Columbia University, people who got between two and four hours of sleep per night had a staggering 73 percent increased risk of obesity; those who got six hours had a 23 percent increased risk.[9]

Some women have the legitimate excuse of sleep interference from others, such as babies, sick children, or their job. Some suffer differing degrees of insomnia. Trouble sleeping was a common complaint of single mothers I interviewed. If you fall into this category, you have options.

- Isolate and understand reasons for stress in your life, and then do what you can to diminish that stress. Start and end your day with prayer.

- Do not eat heavily after seven PM. Look at the pictures of your organs again. Many of them work hardest during the night shift. When your body enters a state of rest and relaxation, they can go to work scrubbing and cleaning. If you have deposited a bag of chips and dip or a heavy dose of meat and potatoes, cleaning will be put to the side while your body deals with digestion.

- Many natural sleep remedies are available on the market. Visit a health food store that has knowledgeable staff and seek their counsel on products.

- Aromatherapy may help. The scent of true lavender, chamomile, or neroli may aid in sleep. (Warning: Many "scents" marketed today are petrochemicals with some sort of smell added. If you are hoping for health effects, be sure your scent is pure.)

- A warm bath (not hot) will help you to come down a notch or two.

- Exercise or hard work during the day can help with sleep. Avoid exercise close to bedtime.

- NO TV, computers, blinking lights, toaster ovens, or waffle makers in the bedroom! The bedroom is a place to sleep. Soft, soothing music, subdued lights if needed for reading, and a darkened room when lights are out all contribute to sleep. We were meant to rest and rejuvenate in the dark, Mom. That's what it's for.

- I am not a fan of sleep medicine. If I was at my wits end, however, and had tried everything natural known to man and just could not sleep, and if my medical doctor kept me under close supervision, I would consider sleep aids once in a while. You have to weigh all the facts before making carte blanche statements. Though sleep is critically important, dependency on sleep medicine is a troublesome possibility when pursuing healthy sleeping patterns.

Let Sleeping Babies Lie

Ah, the kids. Bedtime. War. It doesn't have to be.

I detest calling any part of our relationship with our children a battle, but Mom, if you let your children walk over you, you have lost the war. Might as well put up your white flag right now and let them dominate your every move.

Your children are going to test you. They know where each button is and how hard to push. Decommission those buttons. If you don't do it now, you will face a problem of epic proportion later when the stakes are much higher than going to sleep when you say.

For young children, establish a nighttime routine and stick to it. Yes, Missy is going to bat her blue eyes at you and use baby talk to convince you to stay until she falls asleep. Yes, Junior is going to rant. Expect it. Just don't cave in and don't rant back. My guess is that after a few nights standing your ground, in spite of their resistance, the children will get the message: You mean business. If you cave in to their demands about staying awake, reading, or whatever, you are a dead duck. And if your child's room has a television set or computer in it, I will personally come to your house and throw a brick through it.

Children need sleep every bit as much as you do. Teens in particular need much sleep. Excellent resources are available to you to help you to stand your ground at bedtime. One book, *Food Fights and Bedtime Battles* offers no-nonsense advice about bedtime rigmarole.[10]

Nutrition and Diabetes

I'm going straight for the jugular by discussing a medical condition that is directly associated with poor nutrition: diabetes.

According to the Centers for Disease Control and Prevention, 45 to 50 million Americans could have diabetes by the year 2050, and the medical community would not likely be able to keep up with numbers that high.[11]

The CDC found that 39 percent of girls and 33 percent of boys aged two and a half to three years are likely to develop diabetes. Percentages soar with Hispanic and African-American children. The World Health Organization estimates that the number of diabetes cases globally will escalate from 140 million to 300 million by 2025.[12]

We need to get this straight: Diabetes is not just about sugar. We have this perception that diabetes means not being able to eat Snickers bars anymore. It is much more than that. Diabetes can lead to stroke, heart attack, blindness, kidney disease, or gangrene and limb amputation.

Diabetes is about putting the wrong "food" (I use this word loosely) into our bodies at the wrong time, about being overweight, and about not exercising. Some people have a predisposition to diabetes, and some are born with this condition. I am not talking about those folks. (Type 1 diabetes is pancreatic failure and requires insulin therapy to prevent death.)

According to the *New England Journal of Medicine,* 25 percent of obese children under ten years have either blatant or pre-adult-onset type 2 diabetes.[13] How many children under ten are considered obese? Too many. Lots of these children are developing chronic degenerative diseases that are typically not seen until people reach 50 or 60 years of age!

Though many parents are beginning to awaken to this national embarrassment, not all parents are willing to do something about childhood obesity because the challenge of correcting eating patterns must begin with them. We need to stop kidding ourselves, stop believing every "new and improved" claim from the food industry, kick the fake foods, and learn about the critical needs of our bodies for nutritionally dense foods.

General Nutrition

I am not a trained professional, and I advise that parents consult certified nutritionists, but here are some commonsense suggestions:

- Find an informed doctor who takes the threat of diabetes seriously.

- Consider caring for yourself your highest priority. Model proper care and include the kids in a family personal-improvement program. Make it all-inclusive and fun.

- Network with friends, start a nutrition club, support each other.

- Eat an abundance of above-ground veggies, along with fruits, seeds, nuts, untreated meats, healthy fats, and fresh eggs. Try to include a lot of colorful veggies and a little protein at every meal. Add veggies to tomato sauce, chili, and macaroni and cheese. I am not into being covert with healthy foods. When we sneak healthy food to children, we enforce the idea that they are distasteful.

- I heartily recommend the book *Nourishing Traditions* by Sally Fallon.[14]

- Stop the low-fat craze! Children, in particular, need correct, healthy fats for growth. Besides, we've been on this low-fat kick for years, so how come obesity is soaring?

- Do not allow a refined oil to darken your door. In our home, we use cold-pressed organic olive oil (for limited cooking use, mostly for dressings and the like); unrefined, pure, organic coconut oil (for sautéing and most other cooking needs); ghee, which is clarified butter (used in some cooking); and tons of organic butter. We would not go near most other oils with a ten-foot pole (including salad dressings) whether they were sold in a health food store or not. For additional information on oil I suggest another book, by Mary Enig and Sally Fallon, called *Eat Fat, Lose Fat*.[15]

- Educate yourself about what goes into the food you serve. Read labels. Call manufacturers and ask them what the term "natural flavors" means. (It usually means the flavoring was concocted in a chemical plant in Jersey.)

- Don't be fooled—even though ingredients are listed by volume, such ingredients as sweeteners are often separated into categories to avoid being listed as the primary ingredient. In a three-inch deep list of ingredients, a popular children's breakfast cereal represented sugar as follows: sugar, sugar with peanuts, molasses, dextrose, corn syrup, fructose.[16] Ah, but you don't give Sugarcoatedfluffios to the children? Okeydokey. How about the ingredients of the "Breakfast of Champions?" In order: whole wheat, sugar, salt, corn syrup, partially hydrogenated soybean oil, brown sugar syrup, natural flavor, trisodium phosphate, freshness preserved by BHT.[17]

- Don't become a fanatic but be consistent and resolute. Who doesn't like to see children's faces light up when a box of donuts comes into the house? I'm not into banning donuts. Or soda pop, for that matter.[18] These goodies can be consumed a few times a year as special treats. But to excuse regular consumption with cheap excuses such as "we are making them happy," "they are kids, after all," and "we don't want to deny them *everything*" is pure folly and escapism from parental responsibility.

- Keep a variety of nutritious foods on the table all the time. Children will eat when they get hungry, they will probably eat what their bodies need, and they will probably eat only as much as their bodies ask for.

- Build your own family food pyramid. Make it on the biggest piece of poster board your fridge can carry, and encourage each child to dictate or to write favorite foods in each pyramid category. The only rules for this exercise are that they must take this exercise seriously, and their favorites must be healthy. (Sugar-laden yogurt is *not* health food!)

- Soy, in nearly all forms, is becoming suspect as a culprit in poor health. For more information, visit www.westonaprice.org.

- Monitor your child's weight and health. Chronic cough? Look into food allergy. Runny nose? Empower the immune system.

- Eliminate or greatly reduce refined foods from your children's lives. If it's not in the house, it's not going to be eaten. Processed foods may seem to be your best friend, but they are one of your child's worst enemies. Consider breakfast cereal, for example. I am not a fan of regular, off-the-shelf, standard boxed cereal for breakfast. Unless it's unrefined, un-puffed, un-flaked, un-sugared, and unadulterated, it shouldn't be in the house even if it is organic. I have several reasons for this opinion, one being the glycemic index of many processed foods. (We would probably be better off if we ate dinner for breakfast. Some other cultures eat hearty meals—or soup—for breakfast.)

Glycemic Index

The glycemic index ranks foods by how swiftly and how much they raise blood sugar. Foods that are highly milled or processed break down more quickly than most of those in their natural state, and the quicker something breaks down, the quicker it hits our blood stream. (This is also true of any juice. Even 100 percent organic juice hits with a wallop when drunk with nothing to offset its insulin spike.) The quicker something hits our bloodstream, the quicker it hits our pancreas. Killer

> *"The greatest increase in sugar consumption during the last two decades is from high fructose corn syrup used in soft drinks, ketchup, and many other fabricated foods aimed at children."* [19]
>
> Sally Fallon

bees. Pancreas in overtime, insulin to the rescue! We have no lingering feeling of being full if what we ate passes through us fast. Shazam: morning slump, hungry, irritable, body craving nutrition.

This doesn't happen when you eat oatmeal. (Real oatmeal, that is, not that weird, processed, sugary, oatmeal-flavored instant stuff.) Our bodies need food for fuel. If I had cereal in the house, anything made of refined grains, or highly processed foods, I would serve them for dinner and would be sure to serve something to balance the insulin demand.

Buying Healthy Food

Lack of good nutrition comes at a price. Listen to the words of a Pulitzer Prize winning journalist in his recent essay on hunger in America:

> Long after malnutrition ends, such children have lower IQs. In adolescence, they score worse than their peers on arithmetic, writing, spatial memory and other cognitive tests. Parents and teachers see in them "more anxiety or depression, social problems, and attention problems," according to a volume of studies compiled in 2000 by the National Research Council and the Institute of Medicine. [20]

For me to promote organic-everything would not be realistic. If you are working two jobs and trying to pay the rent, I'm not going to tell you to waltz into the big organic chain store and blow what little you have on free-range chicken. Besides, finding healthy foods in health food stores is getting harder these days...but that's another book. Here is what I suggest:

- Let's start with chicken. If you buy battery chicken (from the big manufacturers and not free range or organic), don't eat the skin or the organs, such as the heart and liver. Cook it properly and safely. Always sanitize everything that came into contact with raw chicken, battery or organic.

- Let's go to the cow. I will not touch hamburger meat unless I know it is organic or I know its source. Sure, we are assured our meat is safe, but that's not the report of such books as *Fast Food Nation*, television documentaries, and increasing voices of concern over the health, slaughter, and processing of our meat and dairy animals.[21] If you do buy nonorganic burger, get the leanest you can because toxins from hormones and antibiotics settle in fattier tissue. Depending on where you live, you may be able to find an inexpensive source of healthy beef. Check with local butchers. Another choice is to avoid ground beef altogether and to buy inexpensive rounds and roasts. Cookbooks abound with recipes for tougher cuts of meat. You say you can't afford to buy a roast? Tell me, how much did it cost you to drive through the fast-food joint the other day, or to buy that latte on the way to work, or to pay for those pizzas? Yet another choice is to eat wild game. Perhaps you know a hunter who would donate deer or elk to your cause. Hunter's freezers are usually crammed.

- Fresh is best; frozen is next to best. Just because something is sold in a produce department does not mean it is fresh. (When buying potatoes and apples, you should always ask, "Is this last year's crop?") If something looks droopy or discolored, avoid it...even if it is organic. The fresher the food, the better for you. You are looking for vibrancy of color and snap, along with heft in weight.

- Please, cut way back on prepared mixes and processed and refined foods.

"You work nonstop, and when you get home you don't
have enough time or energy to do anything but make
half-synthetic processed food in the microwave."

Colleen Huber, Naturopath

Preparing Food

Take an enormous burden out of daily meal preparation by
knowing in advance what you will cook by category. This is merely a
take on the old "Monday is wash day" routine. But in your home, let
Monday be "soup day," as it is in ours. Let me share the categorical
system Joe and I have in our home.

Monday: We have soup for all three meals. We regard Monday as a
"cleaning and resting" day for our organs, and we relish the different
flavors and textures of nutritious broths and soups. You could include
chili or stew in this routine. Soup for breakfast? You bet. Works in Japan.
Soup in a Thermos with hearty buttered bread is good for lunch.

Tuesday: International night. No sense having awesome cookbooks
if we don't use them. Indian and Thai cooking appeal to us lately, and
on Tuesdays our kitchen smells sublime from all those spices. You
might consider Tuesday as "theme night" and encourage the children
to help with decorating the table and learning about different cultures.
Use whole grain tortillas for lunch wraps.

Wednesday: Beef night. We are meat eaters, but we eat small
portions. One steak cut into pieces is ample for us. (Food will seem
to increase like magic when you cut it into pieces before you serve
it.) Learn how to make a good, old-fashioned meat loaf. I've yet to
meet a kid who didn't like meat loaf. A meat loaf sandwich makes a
fabulous lunch.

Thursday: This is our upside-down day. Though we tend not
to eat traditional breakfast foods in the morning, Thursday night
is "breakfast for dinner." Waffles come to mind, made of our own
sourdough starter and accompanied by wild blueberries. You might

have pancakes with fresh whipped cream and berries. School lunch? Hard-boiled eggs and veggies.

Friday: Fish night. Always aware that we don't eat enough fish, we have dedicated a night to this cause. Our fish is usually wild salmon, prepared in a multitude of ways. Though we are concerned about mercury from eating too much tuna, an occasional tuna casserole might be a child-friendly meal. Or fish cakes. When I was young, we often ate codfish cakes on Friday night. Use canned salmon instead of tuna for sandwiches.

Saturday: Free-for-all and use-things-up night. Saturdays are sometimes restaurant nights as well.

Sunday: The Sunday table. Oh, bring it back! Eat at a beautifully prepared table and surround yourself with family and friends. Our three PM Sunday meals are always open to others. We don't care if plates came from the Dollar Store or if we're serving inexpensive Italian (spaghetti). The celebration and the feasting on community is what matters to us. A turkey bought on sale, an inexpensive pot roast, a barbecue...make the Lord's Day special.

Prep Tips

- When unsure about what to have for dinner, first look to the most perishable items in the fridge. What is getting "long in the tooth?" Use it! Turn to a cookbook and find an easy recipe that incorporates that ingredient.

- Don't waste! If something can't be eaten, freeze it. If you can't freeze it, turn it into a smoothie or into soup...then freeze it.

- Cook once and eat twice, or cook big and freeze small. To do this you must keep your freezer organized and use what you have. If you are smart, you will cook two or three times as much of your favorite meals and freeze meal-sized portions. Merely reach into the freezer the night before for your next day's meal, which you can supplement with steamed greens or whole fruits.

- I am not a fan of cooking all your monthly or weekly meals at one time because not that many women I've spoken to are that organized. A well-stocked freezer, however, is every woman's best friend. Certain tasks cut down future food prep significantly, such as preforming meatballs or hamburgers before freezing, breaking down family packs of meats and freezing meal-size portions, or freezing pre-chopped veggies that you might use in stir-fry.

- Practice hospitality. Try to have someone besides your family join you for a few meals each week. You will amaze yourself with how efficient you will feel, how nutritious your meals will be, and how blessed you will be to have the company of others.

Don't Cook at All

Meals needn't be cooked. Here are some suggestions for no-cook meals:

- Have a sandwich bar. Spread all kinds of sandwich ingredients on the table.

- Have antipasto. This is a favorite in the Yates home! Empty the fridge of everything you can find to put on a platter: pickles, olives, cheeses, raw veggies, fruits, meats, artichoke hearts. Drain a can of garbanzo beans. Serve hearty bread with olive oil to dip.

- Enjoy banana splits or yogurt parfaits. Use whole, plain yogurt and flavor and sweeten at home.

- Have a salad bar. Simulate your favorite restaurant salad bar. Include deviled eggs—an easy dish for children to prepare.

Healthy Snack Ideas

- Sliced banana topped with organic nut butter.
- Sliced apple topped with organic nut butter.
- Celery filled with cream cheese and cut into one-inch pieces.

- Smoothies. Add fruit to a plain, healthy yogurt base.
- Trail mix: walnut pieces, raisins or dried fruit, chocolate chips, coconut. (Beware of choking hazard.)

Someone's in the Kitchen with Mama

Engage your children. If you bring them to the market with you, give them a lesson on purchasing healthy produce, determining ingredients by reading labels, and purchasing within a budget. The rewards of cooking and baking with your children are off the charts. If you include your children in cooking for others, you will teach them the gift of hospitality.

Be especially creative. Cookie cutters are an absolute must when preparing food with children. Use them to cut out favorite animals. I do this to wide-eyed excitement with bread, frittatas, and pancakes.

Sacred space. I write about the importance of the family table with love and encouragement. Your family table—whether in the kitchen, in a formal dining room, or on the patio—is arguably the most sacred spot in your home. It is sacred because this is where you come together to share common meals and to break bread. Sadly, in many homes the family table is covered by clutter, and community is cut short by a mad dash to grab the TV remote with plates and bowls balanced on laps. Please, Mom, don't let this be normal behavior for you and your children. Insist that certain meals will be eaten together as a family at the table.

_____ RESOURCES _____

Dr. Joseph Mercola, author of *Dr. Mercola's Total Health Program,* offers a free e-newsletter with information regarding health, medicine, nutrition, mental health, and exercise. Heartily recommended. (www. mercola.com)

The Weston A. Price Foundation is a nonprofit organization dedicated to demonstrating the value of consuming nutrient-dense whole foods found in traditional diets. Some of its information seems counterintuitive because of the information we have received through the media for decades, but this particular approach to health has been highly beneficial to me and my family. I earnestly and sincerely encourage you to investigate the scientific findings of this group and consider them for your family. (www.westonaprice.org)

READING

Eric Schlosser, *Fast Food Nation* (New York: Perennial, 2002).

Carol Simontacchi and Jeremy P. Tarcher, *The Crazy Makers: How Food Industry Is Destroying Our Brains and Harming Our Children* (New York: Putnam, 2000).

Sari Harrar, ed., *The Sugar Solution* (Emmaus, PA: Rodale, Inc., 2004).

Sally Fallon, *Nourishing Traditions: The Cookbook that Challenges Politically Correct Nutrition and the Diet Dictocrats* (Winona Lake, IN: New Trends Publishing, 1999).

Mary Enig and Sally Fallon, *Eat Fat, Lose Fat* (New York: Hudson Street Press, 2005).

Timothy Jordan, *Food Fights and Bedtime Battles* (New York: Berkley Books, 2001).

Eight

Child Care

Children, particularly young children, belong with their mothers.
Many people disagree with that statement. I've encountered
books and articles galore exonerating women from fundamental
responsibility toward their children. Many voices promote child care
apart from Mom as early socialization that is good and progressive
since children learn to stand on their own two feet. For mothers and
children to have routine separation is healthy, they say. That is folly,
and you and I both know it.

But you have to work. I know. What I just wrote was not intended
to heap coals on your head or to burden you but to affirm what
you feel in your heart. You are right, Mom, to yearn to be with your
children. That you cannot be with them is the true burden. (If you
were fabulously wealthy and yet hired a nanny to care for your kids,
I'd feel like coming after you with a Wiffle Bat and knocking some
sense into your head.)

As we go forward and look at child care options, I want to make the strongest case I can for your child's need for you. Motherhood is not a trial run. I exhort you to try to be in place for your children—especially if they are young. Provide stability and security for them and nurture them. Never forget that you are the first and foremost teacher your children will ever have.

Please do everything you can to manage this if you can. If you have to work, ideally you could work at home part of each week or manage on flex hours so your child is primarily in your care. Our daughter-in-law, for instance, worked one long day each week and had overnight responsibilities with her on-call occupation. This minimal separation was a good system as she sacrificially worked while our son was completing his doctorate. Child care needs on her one long workday were met by the now infamous grandmother-in-residence *(moi)* or a private babysitter who was well acquainted with the children.

If you must work and cannot primarily care for your children, the next level of care you should try to find is within your family pool. Are grandparents willing and able to care for the children? Who better than a grandparent to protect them, to teach them, to wipe their noses, and sing to them? Grandparents are safe, reliable, and the next-best caregivers. Turn to your family for help.

> *Be positively certain about the character of the person into whose care you put your children, as well as the character of people who may frequent the care giver's homes. This applies to every single child care provider, right down to grandparents.*

Some older children may sometimes be of help in child care. The duty of care was assigned to me when I was old enough. I cared for my two younger sisters, but I was—at times, mind you— a poor choice for this task. (Sheila and Annie will never let me forget the time I put Brylcreem rather than whipped cream on their Jell-O —a mean-spirited prank I will never live down.) Children of single parents often bear responsibility sooner, and this may be a good thing.

If your family enjoys solidarity by caring for each other and looking out for each other, and if a genuine warmth exists between siblings, a mature enough older child can be of incalculable help.

If no grandparent, relative, or older child is available, perhaps a retired neighbor or stay-at-home friend would be willing to care for your children in your absence.

As I mentioned in chapter 4, you might consider approaching your church to see if they have programs (or willing people) who can volunteer child care services on a regular basis or in a pinch.

Mommy Co-op

If you are able to arrange for creative work time through flex hours, your needs for child care might not be weeklong. You may be able to establish a working arrangement with one or two other mothers who need day care for their children. In this case, you might volunteer to care for others' children in exchange for their care of your child. Needless to say, lots of conversation and planning must go into this arrangement, not to mention the certainty that your children will be safe.

If all else fails, you can turn to governmental, business, and private programs.

I heartily recommend the purchase of *What to Expect Baby-Sitter's Handbook* by Heidi Murkoff with Sharon Mazel.[1] This fabulous resource is filled with valuable information for those who care for your child, with pages of charts that you can complete to customize care. The handbook includes forms that list emergency numbers and the like. A must have—and an excellent new-baby gift.

> *Make all plans for summer child care in the winter!*

Government Services: Head Start

The government has programs called Head Start and Early Head Start—comprehensive child-development programs that serve children from birth to age five, pregnant women, and their families. They are child-focused programs and are designed to increase the school readiness of children in low-income families. Migrant Head Start and American Indian–Alaskan Native Head Start programs are also available. Call your local Health and Human Services Agency to find a Head Start program near you.

Your municipality may offer day care for special-needs children.

The Big Business of Day Care

You may be fortunate to work where care is provided for children on the premises, or your place of employment may allow you to occasionally bring your child to work if this causes no disruption in the work environment. This may happen when a child is home due to snow days or other no-school days.

Finding a day care facility that you can afford and trust is a big hurdle. On their website, the American Academy of Pediatrics recommends you consider several things when searching for day care. I summarize them here:[2]

Child to staff ratio. Does each adult have too many children to handle? Licensing guidelines usually cover this matter, but a good ratio is one adult caregiver for every six to eight young children and one caregiver to every ten to fourteen older children.

Separation by age. Are the children all lumped into one or two rooms, or are they separated according to age and development?

Discipline policies. Are specific policies in place for discipline and other issues? Are these policies in writing, and are they available to you?

Care of sick children. How is medicine given, how are parents notified about illness among the children, and what constitutes a medical reason to keep your child at home? Is a separate sick room available, and are medical records kept for each child?

Staff training. How has the staff been trained? Do any staff have specific training to identify abuse? Do any staff have degrees in child development and the like? Is all of the staff trained in first aid and child CPR?

Hygiene. Is hand washing mandated, and do the adults and children actually do it? Does the building look clean, does it smell, and does the building or the playground appear to be dangerous in any way?

Your child. If your child already is enrolled in day care, ask him or her how the day went, if anything unusual happened, and what he or she did.

Red Flags

Insufficient answers. If your questions to the day care are not answered sufficiently, press for answers and be as articulate as you can when questioning. If you remain dissatisfied with the response, ask again in writing and expect a written response. Remain cordial, these people are busy. A good day care will respond favorably.

Your involvement. Are you discouraged from participating or volunteering at the day care? If it seems secretive and off-limits, investigate the reason why.

Unhappy kids. If your child is moody, angry, unhappy, or reluctant to attend day care (other than usual child behavior), consider this a warning sign and learn why.

Accidents. If you hear of accidents or mishaps regularly, this may be a sign of poor adult supervision.

Staff turnover. If staff members change often, this too is worth investigating. If working conditions are poor, children may suffer.

Caution from others. Take seriously any warning from other parents about a day care you are considering. Reputation matters.

YMCA

The YMCA is the nation's largest nonprofit community service organization. It works to meet the health and social service needs of millions of men, women, and children in thousands of communities in the United States and abroad. Their child care fees are typically 30 percent lower than the national average, and their website states that "no one is turned away for inability to pay." The Y offers child care, school-age care, and teen programs. About 40 percent of the children in YMCA child care come from single-parent homes. From swimming lessons to drug abuse prevention to family nights to basketball, if you are fortunate to have a nearby YMCA, the opportunities seem endless. Check your local phone book for a YMCA in your town, or visit www.ymca.net to find a Y near you.

The Dreaded Snow Day or Sick Day

You have to be at work, and Missy has the mumps. What to do?

- Have a backup plan ahead of time. Either know for sure that you can call upon family or friends or church members, or make sure your boss will let you take off rather abruptly on occasion.

- Investigate home-based or center-based care centers for mildly sick children in your town and visit those premises ahead of time. Look for (and smell) sure signs of neglect or insufficient sanitation and hygiene. Ask what kind of arrangements can be made should you need their services.

- Regardless of who cares for your child, be doubly sure that you leave a detailed written explanation for any medicine: dose, time to administer, whether to give with food or not, if it must be refrigerated. Expect a full report in return.

Without turning this event into some sort of holiday, if your child is sick enough to stay home, make the stay pleasant and comfortable. I've read child-development experts who insist that if the child is sick enough to stay home, he or she is too sick to watch TV. I understand the rationale behind this, though I do not fully agree. While rest is necessary for the body to heal, a little TV may help the day pass easier. Provide comfort food for the child, and consider keeping a special pair of pajamas just for sick occasions. Keep the child calm and quiet.

After School

Statistics aren't too rosy for the older child who is left alone after school until Mom comes home. The author of a book called *Home Alone America* has the fortitude to examine the hard data about the effects absent parents have on childhood development.[3]

I about lost it when I read a recent article in *Reader's Digest,* and not because of the alarming statistics the author presented about what "kids are up against when they must fend for themselves," and not because the author said that recent research "paints a bleak picture." What got me was the last line in the article, when an "expert" is quoted as saying: "In the final analysis, it's really not the amount of time you spend, but the quality."[4] It's as if the article's author wrote page after page that "red is red is red is red" and ended her piece with "red is blue." Anyway, didn't we discredit that quality vs. quantity nonsense long ago?

If you can't be at home after school, find someone who can. If you can't find someone who can, find someplace for your child to go, such as extracurricular activities or a safe home with adult supervision. If none of the above is possible, establish a monitoring system whereby the child reports to you and accounts for time spent alone. Technology exists to protect them from certain TV or Internet exposure. A bond of trust is key between you and your children to pull this off if your child is unattended and alone.

This is a good time to talk about trust. Nothing is wrong with trusting your child's character while not trusting your child's judgment.

Incidentally, finding after-school activities may not be too hard. According to a recent survey, about 80 percent of middle and high school students participate in organized activities after school and on weekends, and 57 percent have something scheduled nearly every day.[5]

Types of activities include sports, drama, school clubs or activities, volunteer work, religious instruction, music and dance lessons and the like, after-school programs, part-time jobs, tutoring, and organizations such as Scouts.

According to an AP article, "Almost nine in ten students agree they need to be pushed by parents into things that are good for them, even if they might complain." Curiously, more than eight in ten students said kids who participate in organized activities were better off than those who have a lot of time to themselves after school.[6]

_____ RESOURCES _____

According to their website, the **Boys and Girls Clubs of America** make a difference in the community by giving young people a safe place to learn and grow. (1-800-854-CLUB, www.bgca.org)

I Have a Dream Foundation motivates and empowers children from low-income communities to reach their educational and career goals by providing a long-term program of mentoring, tutoring and enrichment, and tuition assistance for higher education. (212-293-5480, www.ihad.org)

The National Association of Child Care Resource and Referral Agencies helps millions of families find, evaluate, or pay for child care each year, providing a bridge between providers, community leaders, and policy makers. In addition, they work with child care providers and families dealing with children exhibiting challenging behaviors. (202-393-5501, www.naccrra.org)

_____ READING _____

Heidi Murkoff, *What to Expect Baby-Sitter's Handbook* (New York: Workman Publishing, 2003). Highly recommended.

Nine

Discipline Through Discipling

"I wish I didn't give in to the nagging. This is such a
learning process, being a mother. It isn't easy."

Dottie

For your information, I have a Clifford the Big Red Dog Band-Aid on my toe, dried baby drool on my shoulder, Kleenex in my pocket, and a diaper in my purse. I tell you this to remind you that I am connected to children and not in some ivory tower pontificating. Neither am I an old fuddy-duddy with prehistoric notions about child care. I am a hands-on grandmother who spends significant time with our three young grandchildren. I also have extensive experience with children of all ages through many years in youth ministry. I frequent places mothers frequent; I go to parks and discovery museums and play areas. I participate, I talk…and I observe. But before I have my say, we should hear from God.

Train a Child

Proverbs 22:6 says to "train a child in the way he should go, and when he is old he will not turn from it." As far as I am concerned, the way is Jesus Christ. All manner of rules, regulations, and behavior must be considered secondary. We must be careful not to confuse this issue.

Our goal is not to bring up well-adjusted, socially responsible, polite kids. Humanists have nice kids. Atheists have nice kids. That is not the issue. The issue is Jesus Christ—our priority, our cornerstone, and our foundation. You, Mom, as Christ's image bearer, are the solid base from which your family's foundation springs. Though adherence to biblical principles will usually turn out citizens who are well-adjusted, responsible, and polite, this is not our priority. Our top priority must be a relational foundation in Jesus—a discipling—cemented firmly in each child's heart. If we push spiritual principles without promoting a relationship with Jesus, we are putting the cart before the horse.

Mom, your children see the real you. Do they see Jesus? Does the power of the Holy Spirit indwell your family life? Are examples of love, joy, peace, patience, kindness, goodness, faithfulness, gentleness, and self-control evident? (See Galatians 5:22-23.) Have children learned through you that they are ultimately responsible to Jesus? Does Jesus have lordship of your home—is He recognized as Savior?

The first step in discipline, therefore, must be discipling children and bringing them to an awareness of a relational God. God gave children families to instill and enforce His Word diligently to them. Children's foundations in Christian faith must be firmly planted.

If they are not, every wind of doctrine and temptation that blows through town will tip them over.

Sand Castles

Time for an illustration. Think of sand castles. People spend hours sculpting a magnificent sand structure, and when the first tide rolls in it's flattened, dissolved in swirling, foamy saltwater. Now think of building blocks. A building-block castle might be shaken by waves, but it will stand, unbudging and barely affected. So with our faith. Unless we have the solid foundation of relationship with Christ, as well as biblical principles and doctrine, firmly cemented in our own minds and hearts, the first wave that rolls in will clobber us. We will be left with nothing but confusion swirling in our heads and soggy, disappearing faith. We simply cannot expect our children to find safe harbor in our "castles" if they are built of sand. Listen to the apostle Paul:

> For we are God's fellow workers; you are God's field, God's building. By the grace God has given me, I laid a foundation as an expert builder, and someone else is building on it. But each one should be careful how he builds. For no one can lay any foundation other than the one already laid, which is Jesus Christ (1 Corinthians 3:9-11).

George Will is a columnist whom I admire. In one of his recent editorials, he examined what I believe to be the folly (and failure) of a segment of our therapeutic culture. He writes about how "sensitivity" protocol is replacing virtue and strength of character that is honed through hardship or difficulty. These therapeutic methods focus on discovering all of one's feelings in the present moment, and

You are building the foundations of your children's lives.

the criteria for all belief and behavior becomes nothing more than an awareness of the child's inner, feeling world. This model concentrates on cushioning emotions from the slightest suggestion of hardship or intimidating environment.

Mr. Will writes, "Because children are considered terribly vulnerable and fragile, playground games like dodge ball are being replaced by anxiety-reducing and self-esteem-enhancing games of tag where nobody is ever 'out.' But abundant research indicates no connection between high self-esteem and high achievement or virtue." He asks the necessary question: "Is not unearned self-esteem a more pressing problem?"[1]

This kind of thinking and subsequent behavior toward children—that nobody is ever wrong, that it's harmful to show criticism or correction, and that we must sugarcoat everything to do with children—is just plain nuts. We learn through mistakes and through correction. If we were flawless, we would not need education, laws, or supervision. To constantly affirm a child when affirmation is not warranted is to do a terrible disservice to that child, who will not grow with positive self-image but with an inflated ego that needs constant reassurance and encouragement. We could be creating emotional cripples. I am not making a case against positive affirmation. More than one source I've read encourages five positive affirmations for each negative criticism. I am a staunch proponent of affirmation—if it is warranted.

Some parents put a stamp of approval on everything their darlings do or say, nary a disapproving or critical comment in sight, and refuse to reprimand or be firm with a child for fear of hurting the child's feelings.

When anyone we know, a child or an adult, does something worthy of acknowledgment, we should hoot, holler, and dance with joy. This kind of positive affirmation and recognition for someone's effort or triumph should be standard operating procedure for all family members. That's what family is for.

Is therapy ever advisable? Yes! Feel-good sentiments aside, some health and safety issues require sound professional counsel and intervention. Self-abuse, addiction, violence, and the like, as well as difficulty coping with changes in family structure, all call for expert advice and help. You would be foolish to think a set of rules or a good heart-to-heart can mediate against such serious issues. My rant about some therapeutic models was toward a trend to do away with healthy competition or necessary constructive criticism.

I am beginning to dislike the word "okay." I climb the wall when I hear parents say something like "I want you to go to bed, okay?" Parents should not complete sentences that involve requests or discipline with the word "okay." This leaves the decision to comply (however semantic) with the child. You're asking, "Do you agree?" I am careful to use "Do you understand?" whenever I make a point with children. This leaves no room for noncompliance; it is a direct command or clear instruction.

Chipped and Worn, but Building Blocks Just the Same

As we've seen, the counsel of Scripture is clear that you are to train your children, and God has equipped you with enough common sense and wisdom to tackle the job. Sure, you'll make mistakes. We all do. I encourage you to study experts in child behavior and development (excluding the "sensitivity" group, please) who will aid you immeasurably. Seek also the counsel of other mothers whose children are already grown. Networking with people who speak your language provides tremendous comfort. And one more thing: Understand that every good intention, every perfect parenting technique, every sacrifice does not guarantee children will march lockstep with projected outcomes and development. Children are sentient beings with wills and personalities—and sometimes with baggage. Do the best you can, hope and pray for the best, and rely on the promise of Proverbs 22. In all things, however, assume your role.

When asked how she disciplines, Sheila, the mother of two teens, had no-nonsense answers:

> Question: How do you discipline?
> Answer: I discuss why to behave and how…and they
> fear the consequences.
>
> Question: What are your strengths?
> Answer: They believe I'll do what I say.

Start Being the Parent

Listen to a single mom from Montana whose children have left the nest: "I'd like for you to tell mothers that they need to stop being best friends and start being parents. If children are always aware of what you will permit and that you will not change from that position, they will appreciate the stability. They won't always agree, but they will appreciate it later, and most will tell you so." Be the parent. Don't be blinded into lax performance by your love or their clever manipulation. She is your daughter, not your best friend; he is your son, not your husband. You will enjoy strong friendship as your children mature into young adults…and what a sense of accomplishment that brings! In the meantime, your kids need an adult in the home—that would be you, and your authority is crucial. Your kids may not agree with everything you say. Let me reword that: Your kids will not agree with everything you say, but they will appreciate the stability you provide them.

Family is the most important thing in a child's life, and your authority is necessary to keep your family from collapsing. As I mentioned before, society has influenced many of us to compromise our authority for the sake of children's feelings and rights. You want to talk rights? Children have a right to be disciplined. If we do not meet the challenge of discipline in our homes, our children will someday pay a great penalty for lessons they never learned. What lessons have you learned, Mom?

One predominant lesson from popular culture is that mothers and fathers cannot be good at parenting unless they love themselves first. That is a lie. Love of self is a lie of the spirit of this age, and it hasn't worked. When is someone going to bring this philosophy to its logical conclusion? Teach everyone to think of themselves first, and we will end up in a shallow paralysis. Selfish love does not have to be taught and should not be enforced; every one of us has a healthy dose of this sentiment already. That's why Jesus told us to love our neighbor as we love ourselves. He knew that our self-love could easily be blown out of proportion. I am convinced that some forms of depression and much of our moodiness and self-pity come directly from love of self as we obsess with ills or hardships that have come upon us. And then we call it low self-esteem! It's more likely a very high level of self-esteem. "Poor me," the sentiment goes.

The Bible gives us a simple formula for self-worth and self-esteem: Die to self, pick up your cross, and follow Christ (Luke 9:23-24). We simply must get off the "me" kick and turn our attention to others, especially if they are little and live with us.

In *Balancing Life's Demands*, J. Grant Howard says this: "Every time you produce another child, you add another top priority responsibility. Children have ongoing, ever-changing needs that parents have to meet...Children need to be played with, read to, talked with, listened to, held close, and as they grow, let go."[2]

Time-Out for Everyone

This is a good place to hear again from Shane, a single mom of three young children. Her advice about time-out for everyone is smart. If you are prone to rash reaction or temper flares, consider taking the time to count to ten or to remove yourself from the situation for a few minutes (or hours or days) so you can make reasoned evaluations or decisions. She explains, "I am guilty of yelling at times and losing my temper. I know it's not a good idea, but sometimes I am so tired and frustrated and nothing is working that I just get fed up. Enough is enough. At those times I just have to say 'Time-out for everybody!' so I can have a few minutes to calm down. When you are the only adult in the house, it can be hard to pull off."

Discipline Through Discipling

Discipling simply means teaching people to be disciples of Jesus Christ. Discipling is what Jesus did in the four gospel accounts as He taught His followers how to follow. Discipling is no different from discipline for a child: You present guidelines and rules as you teach your children to behave.

I repeat: You set the standards, not the child. You are the parent. Your children depend on you to act like one. The only time your children are living in a democracy is when you're voting on which movie to rent on Saturday night.

Discipline does not mean punishment, though punishment in the form of isolation, reparation, or denial can be a part of discipline. Discipline means establishing limits and parameters and enforcing them through continuous reinforcement and repetition. It means kindness and respect. (If you ever use the words "shut up" with your children, I will hunt you down with that Wiffle Bat!)

Discipline means listening. I positively implode when I hear children's comments go unacknowledged. At all costs, acknowledge your children—even if they are three and filled with redundant questions. Never turn a deaf ear. Let them know you heard their comment, even if you have to put them on hold for a while.

Discipline means having expectations and declaring what you expect from your children. It means never expecting perfection but asking that your children strive toward perfecting important virtues. Make a written set of rules and post them where they can serve as a reminder. Writing rules creates a clear framework that communicates what will be an acceptable or unacceptable practice. Communicating rules for behavior inside and outside the household is necessary. No gray areas. Reinforcement and reminders are standard operating procedure when dealing with children. Establish methods to communicate with one another in every manner possible. Write notes, call each other, keep a calendar, and develop signals.

Age-Appropriate Discipline

You do not have to condone negative behavior just because it is typical. For instance, perhaps you read in a child-development book that children typically say no and scream when they are two. So your child throws fits, screams, and disrupts the house, and you say to yourself, *This is normal,* and let the behavior continue. Let's fast-forward to the teenage years and look at some "normal" development, shall we? Are you going to condone drugs or sexual experimentation because, well, shoot—kids that age do that sort of thing? Yeah, right.

Ah, but we say, children may act out due to inner turmoil. Of course children act out...they are children, remember? Your job is to teach them that regardless of their turmoil, regardless of their age, some behavior is inappropriate. This is how they learn self-control, which, by the way, is part of the fruit of the Spirit.

More from Shane: "My leniency continued through the divorce. I felt it was my fault the kids had to suffer through that. Once the divorce was final and I was trying to get back on track, the kids fought me tooth and nail because they were so used to getting away with everything. I don't think I've ever gotten the discipline under control."

Discipline in an age-appropriate way. A common recommendation is time-out should last one minute per age of the child. I've seen this practice work extremely well; none of us likes to be isolated. I've also seen it used so often it became a ho-hum experience.

Keep in mind that each child is different and that you should apply sense and reason to any rules you apply. Don't go around issuing fiats without showing the consideration to explain why you are enacting such rules. "You may not have friends over when I am not home" is a fiat—and a very good one, I might add. A fiat with the added consideration of reason and fairness might sound like this: "You may not have friends over when I am not home because...

- I trust your integrity and honesty, but until you are older I cannot yet trust your judgment.

- I trust you but have no reason to trust others.

- The probability of doing something you shouldn't increases significantly when someone else encourages such behavior.

- I am ultimately responsible for any liability.

- I am uncomfortable with the idea of other kids in the house without supervision.

- This is in keeping with my other decision—that you don't go to other friend's homes when their parents are not home.

Also keep in mind that regardless of how essential the discipline, you never, ever need to inflict pain on a child. (Abject misery when "the world is coming to an end" because of a grounding is not what I mean by pain.) And as I stated before, verbal abuse can be as painful as the business end of a belt.

> "An unattended kid is a recipe for disaster."
> *Marcie*
> _____

Family Mission Statement

What does your family stand for? I dare say few of us have ever stopped to think about this. Establishing your overall direction and purpose is a very good idea because you are, after all, the most important social structure in the world. In one of his excellent books, James Stenson writes, "Serious reflection about your mission and your children's future will give you purposeful direction for your family life, and this will embolden you to plan and to act effectively."[3] If your children are old enough to participate, by all means include them when you write your family mission statement. If they are not old enough to comprehend, write one by yourself. Here's an example of a family's mission statement:

> As a family we are united in our determination to live godly lives, to love, defend, and support each other, to reach out to those less fortunate, and to always bring glory to God.

Try writing a family mission statement here:

_____

_____

_____

Teaching Your Kids Discernment

One mother says, "Christian parents should constantly teach and remind their children so they can identify the evil in the world...so that they have the tools to combat it." Like this mother, I believe that discipling must include discernment. In Christian terms, discernment simply means telling the difference between what Jesus taught and what others teach. This applies to your household environment and your kids' ability to distinguish between what you expect and stand for and other families' standards. Children must learn discernment very early on. Along with this, however, comes a caution.

On one hand, we must take care that we do not create an unnatural paranoia in the hearts of our little ones, and we must be absolutely certain we do not make midget Pharisees out of them. We have a duty to be in the world but not of it, but too many people have practiced a form of spiritual snobbery rather than Christian love. On the other hand, we don't want our kids to grab tightly onto the world's values. (More on this in the next chapter.) Nor do we want them to become complacent about their faith.

Christian children should be taught this time-tested response to questionable practices or behavior: When in doubt, don't! If children of any age come home with an unsettled feeling when facing difficult or marginal situations, you have a golden opportunity to discuss the source of their doubt: the discerning of God the Holy Spirit. Qualify and edify the work of the Holy Spirit in your child's life.

Discipline from Others

Enforcing your family rules when other people are temporarily in custody and supervising your children is quite another matter. In a nutshell, I'm talking about the children's father or other family members. Single mothers the world over are stressed because of other people's noncompliance to their rules and nutritional standards. More than one mother was furious as they described how their ex-husbands acted like Peter Pan to the children, making the mothers look (and feel) like Captain Hook.

It may be that you (yes, you) will have to be the one to heroically sidestep your fury and try, try again to have reasoned conversation with the children's father about their upbringing. Try using the principle of ownership we talked about in chapter 3. Set a time for an uninterrupted meeting and go determined to *not* respond to his stimuli as you always have. (If you communicated okay, you probably wouldn't be divorced.) Your cool and peaceful response may be enough to get him to listen. Use some openers like these:

- I'm glad we can come together to review the progress our children are making.

- The children love to be with you, and I appreciate the time and energy you put into your relationship. How do you think we can work together to make this transition from home to home and back again relatively seamless?

- What do you think we should do about Tommy's lack of attention to schoolwork?

- Do the children seem overstimulated when they are with you? What do you think we should do about that?

If your earnest effort to establish harmony in this area falls on deaf ears, do what you can to explain to the children that they should honor your rules within reason when they are in someone else's care. You do not want to create tension in the children and may have to chalk this up to the way it is while doing your best when they are with you.

Kids are often tempted to play both ends against each other in order to get their way. "Dad lets me…" "Mom says we can…" A copy of your family rules should be posted on Dad's fridge too, whether he complies with them or not.

READING

James Dobson, *The New Strong-Willed Child* and *The New Strong-Willed Child Workbook* (Colorado Springs: Focus on the Family, 2005).

Paul C. Reisser, *The Complete Book of Baby and Child Care* (Carol Spring, IL: Tyndale Publishing, 1999).

Ten

Cultural Bombardment and Peer Pressure

"It's as if aliens came and carted my real son away."

Marcie

The Spirit of the Age

Parents have always worried about their young. Fortunately, for almost two centuries, the American way of life shared many values with the home. A working partnership between family and society stood in place. Universal principles affected many aspects of our culture and government. But since the cultural revolution of the 1960s, we've heard a new cry: "Down with the old, and bring on the new!"

In many ways, our country is destabilized and uncertain about its future drift. Established mores are up for grabs as values and beliefs turn upside down. Scripture says, "Woe to those who call evil good and good evil, who put darkness for light and light for darkness" (Isaiah 5:20). This country is abandoning traditional behavior and blasting into the newness of change whether we like it or not. Questions hang in the balance:

Will change be moderated by old, accustomed values? Will Christians have a place in a new society? Will our children survive the onslaught of philosophies that are hostile to biblical instruction?

Parents absolutely must become and remain informed about what is happening in popular culture, in the schools, on TV, and over the Internet. Children are soaking up staggeringly base cultural mores that hit them like fast food on Saturday night. Everything is up for grabs.

Change can create chaos; confusion often abounds when change is in the air. And confusion neutralizes people faster than anything I know. Rather than face a bewildering challenge, or deal with proposed reform, many people tend to sidestep issues and join an ever increasing fellowship of fence sitters.

In the meantime, much seems to be chaotic. Man has become God, right has become wrong, objectivity has become subjectivity, and no has become "Why not?" Enter spiritual confusion as the enemy of our souls gets people to shake their heads and mutter, "To each his own." How great for Satan that confusion neutralizes! When faith is neutralized, people of faith are no longer productive for the kingdom of God. Without faith to sustain them they are bombarded by cultural mandate.

Where do you stand, single mom? Can you and will you defend the holiness of your household against cultural bombardment?

When we think of cultural bombardment, we usually think of fighting a battle "out there," and we brace ourselves against the wiles of the world without recognizing that the world has brought its message in living color, surround sound, and slick print into our private lives. Television, music, magazines, books, DVDs, computer games, toys, and fashion all impact the fabric of our lives and influence our moral and religious sway.

Television and the Holiness of Your Household

"Do not bring a detestable thing into your house or you, like it, will be set apart for destruction. Utterly abhor and detest it, for it is set apart for destruction" (Deuteronomy 7:26).

Have you allowed anything in your home that would grieve the heart of God? Let me ask you this: What do you allow your children to watch on TV? What do you watch? Never mind that "I'm an adult" rhetoric...does it hurt the heart of God or not? Do you really believe gratuitous sex and violent programming is okay because you are over eighteen?

> "The way Christians and morality are portrayed on TV
> absolutely disgusts me."
>
> *Marcie*

This is the promised other side of the coin from my previous (cautious) endorsement of wise TV use. Many people have cautioned that, when left unchecked, television is turning many of our children into a mindless generation. Lacking cognitive stimulation, children become less able to react effectively to the simplicity of life without high drama and excitement. "Bored" has hit new meaning in our culture and now means, "I want some action—stimulate me!" Have you seen this in children you know? TV viewing has other consequences.

A study of hundreds of four-year-olds elicited the following statistics: Children were 25 percent more likely to become bullies if they watched the average daily amount of TV—three and a half hours. Children who watched eight hours of TV a day were 200 percent more likely to become bullies.[1] The American Academy of Pediatrics sees TV as such a threat to our children that they recommend no TV for children under two!

Dr. Carl Pickhardt says, "TV, video and computer games may contribute to ADD/ADHD behavior by delivering exciting stimulation in extremely short and varied bursts, constantly and quickly changing the child's focus, brain-training the child to need excessive stimulation and to have an increasingly short attention span."[2]

Study after study shows that behavior is linked to television, yet some people continue to haughtily proclaim, "I don't let what's on TV affect me."

Please. Do you mean to tell me that the average person who reaches 18 in this country, who has watched thousands of hours of television and has seen hundreds of thousands of commercials, as well as countless murders and acts of sex, hasn't in any way been affected by any of it? Then why do advertisers spend millions on commercials?

No problem, we say! We'll watch family friendly shows! Ever watch the Olympics? Great family entertainment. Suspense...drama... commercials...and previews for upcoming violent adult programming. You can't be too careful, Mom.

Some of us are willing to compromise values for the sake of entertainment. Yet if we are serious about protecting our children, we are going to have to do some serious praying about the issue of TV.

The question of TV is the same as for anything else we bring into the house: Does it edify the family, promote God's values, and please His Holy Spirit? If you choose to keep your television set, at least commit yourself to watch what your children watch. Some parents feel strongly that TV should be allowed in moderation (I agree), and they monitor time spent watching allowable programs. Technology (the V-chip) exists to control channel selection when you are not home.

Suggestions for Television Use

- Mute all commercials or tape programs and fast-forward through commercials.
- Watch TV with your children and take time to explain the difference between the way of the world and God's way.
- Watch a program with your child and encourage the child to alert

you to spiritual dangers in programming and commercials. Use this as a tool for in-depth conversation. Help the child to develop discernment and the ability to make spiritual distinctions. Help your children get through the humor, the intrigue, or the action and find the message.

- Have house rules that govern the use of TV, as well as time limits, such as no TV or TV limited to specific programs on school nights.

- Allow children a certain block of TV time each week, and let them choose from acceptable programming.

- No TV in anyone's bedroom. Ditto computers.

- Get rid of television altogether.

- Don't use television privileges as a reward or punishment...it makes it too important.

The Internet

What if you found out your child is surfing the Net to find porn?

If I had my way, TVs or computers would not be allowed in children's bedrooms. Beyond moral and predatory dangers, I believe the electromagnetic field they emit presents a health hazard that none of us should be sleeping in. TV and Internet misuse is simply too much temptation for a child or teen to responsibly cope with.

Chat rooms on the Internet have been ripe hunting grounds for child predators. As I stated earlier, you may trust your child's earnest intent to live a godly life, but you cannot—you must not—trust your child's judgment.

Some evil people are in this world, and you must shield your children in every manner possible. Check with your Internet provider for technology to shield your children on the Internet by blocking objectionable sites, spam, and advertising.

Computers are excellent and vital tools. They can open a door to the world and be at your service. It is up to you to be sure they don't open a door to evil strangers.

While we're dealing with computer technology, let me add my two cents about cell phones. If affordable, they can be a boon to the single mom by keeping a direct line to her children. Based on my research, however, I feel that cell phones post a serious health risk at this time. Please check this further at Dr. Joseph Mercola's free Web newsletter at www.mercola.com. Search for "cell phones."

Music

Young people listen to lyrics over headphones for hours on end. Music is an effective communicator and teacher. (Just think of the toddler's ABC song.) But much popular music promotes activity that is blatantly and expressly opposed to Christian values and morality. When kids listen to songs repeatedly, the messages permeate the subconscious like quick-rise yeast in pizza dough. Music in a teen's life comes second to having friends, and kids spend nearly as much time listening to music as they do at school. We shrug this off as some sort of developmental mandate or relent and buy offensive CDs when our kid throws a fit. Pat, the mother of three teens, stays on top of media influence as best she can: "I need to know what my children are feeding their minds with."

No one would deny that music is important, but certain types of music must be denied. Prayer and open conversation must attend your decision to ban certain music in your home. Be reasonable but be responsible. This is a tough and touchy area in any teen's life and requires sensitivity as well as sensibility. Music that opposes the kingdom of God must be prohibited.

Suggestions for Music Listening

- Children love music. Purchase the classics and let some of the more exciting pieces thunder through your home. The *1812 Overture* would be good for this.

- Music is expressive. Younger children particularly love to dance and jump to the rhythm. Encourage children to creatively respond to the sound of music...hmmm...*The Sound of Music!* Excellent choice!

- We often listen to sounds and not to lyrics. Ask your children what songs mean, or ask them to sing the song to you. Lyrics are printed in CD liners.

- Create an orchestra with kitchen utensils. Get silly with younger kids. Create your own music or play along with a favorite song. Imagine the joy of a youngster if Mom is on the kitchen floor with a pot and a wooden spoon!

- Encourage music lessons or voice lessons if the child is so inclined.

- So what if the teenagers take up all the room in your house with their musical instruments? Give kids the freedom to exercise their talents, and encourage them to explore the great joy of musical expression.

- Don't deny good Christian rock that edifies the Lord.

- Teach your children that music is calming as well as stimulating. They should learn to appreciate soft music too.

- Encourage older kids to join band or choir in school.

- Encourage your church to have a kids' choir to integrate the children into the service.

> "Keep those little bodies busy. Dancing lessons, music lessons, drama, church youth group, sports...Keep the positive influences coming."
>
> *Marcie*

Magazines

Teen magazines are hooked on hedonism. They provocatively present the female body ad nauseum. From fingernails to split ends, young girls are told repeatedly they must be perfect, and heaven help them if they are not. Celebrities become cultural icons and trend setters. Women's magazines promote celebrities who have had a series of partners and exemplify worldly values. Magazine profiles present this behavior as normal and even enviable. Many of the magazines we bought when we were young have changed to fit the trends and lifestyles of our culture, which is hot for self-approval and self-love. For a healthy alternative, Focus on the Family has an amazing assortment of excellent magazines for kids of all ages.

Beware, Mom. If we continue to suggest that kids must cater to the flesh and seductively perfect it, we are going to end up with even more cases of eating disorders as impressionistic minds try vainly to join a sexually liberated "size six and under" generation. This brings me to the matter of clothing.

Clothing

Seductively dressed children and teens do not make a good Christian witness. Neither do little girls who dress beyond their age. Nor do children who are walking advertisements for evil. This doesn't mean you should dress your kids in shrouds and deny them current fashion. Just be sure the fashion statement your child is making doesn't go too far. (By the way, same for you, Mom.)

Please, put some common sense into the way you allow your children to dress. Teach them that indecent clothing is disrespectful of our bodies, which are temples of the Holy Spirit. Fads are okay and to be expected, but don't let your child's clothing offend God. (While I'm on the subject, one of my pet peeves is how slovenly we dress for church.)

Too much love won't spoil a child, but too few limits will.

Children as Consumers

Children are very big business. Marketers for everything from hair gel to fruit leather spend staggering amounts of money for ads that target kids (backed by expensive studies to understand the child and teenage psyche). There are very good reasons for this.

For one thing, according to a study by market researchers Packaged Facts, not only do families with 3- to 12-year olds spend $53.8 billion annually on entertainment, personal care items, and reading materials for their children, children themselves have discretionary money which they spend liberally. In 2003 alone, teens spent roughly $175 billion on themselves.[3]

Besides tapping into this lucrative market, companies are banking on establishing "cradle to grave" brand loyalty. Creating loyalty in a person for a particular logo or brand while they are young is shrewd if businesses want to stay in the game. In a telling column, Courtland Milloy interviewed young men about their determination to acquire a certain basketball shoe. Mr. Milloy writes, "And so it went at select shoe stores…customers who called ahead were advised to show up at least an hour before the store opened at 7 AM Sunday. The line began forming in the cold of dawn, and before the sun could break through the morning fog, all…were gone." When one fellow was informed that the $160 sneaker probably cost $2 to manufacture, his response was, "I don't care if they cost a penny to make. These are Jordans." This sentiment was typical.[4]

Marketers are targeting your children for their money. They use everything from science to teen focus groups to determine how to get that money. One way they get it is to create need in children: the need to belong, to be accepted, to feel the power associated with the name. Though we are not one bit different than the kids, we are at least wise to the game. (Or at least we should be.)

Children—and especially teens—face profound pressure to fit in. (Odd that most kids rebel against the status quo yet march lockstep to status quo pressure and demands of their peers.) Kids want to be "in," and having the latest in fashion, technology and music is their way of establishing equality with their peers. It is a leveler. In a recent commercial for an absurdly big and ugly SUV, a shy little boy is carted to school, only to gain instant status and respect by students when he emerges from the car (or whatever it is called). The commercial's message was clear and unmistakable: What you ride in matters. Self-worth and esteem come from things, not from within. It's all show, baby.

Though wanting to fit in is normal, the motivating force behind it is destructive: Covetousness has never been a favorable behavior. Nor has greed. Want to hear from God again? "When you ask, you do not receive, because you ask with wrong motives, that you may spend what you get on your pleasures. You adulterous people, don't you know that friendship with the world is hatred toward God? Anyone who chooses to be a friend of the world becomes an enemy of God" (James 4:3-4).

As I've already mentioned, I feel we are hurting our children by allowing them to have too much too soon. Our wise parenting must teach kids to say not to immediate gratification, or our kids are in for bumpy roads ahead. As James B. Stenson says, "If children do not experience loving denial, they cannot form the concept of self-denial. To arrive at adolescence these days without a well-formed internal power of self-denial is positively dangerous."[5] The way we teach children that happiness lies in consumption is a national disgrace.

Kids' rooms are cluttered with "must-haves"—so much that children are overwhelmed and find no real lasting enjoyment from toys. Mom, teach your children the great lesson of simplicity and satisfaction.

Yet another problem with our consumptive society is that marketers now set many of the social, cultural, and normative concepts of childhood as younger and younger children make purchasing decisions. Let me ask again: Who is the parent? Who should be setting standards for your children, especially those that relate to body image or finances—you or Disney? Let me also ask, Where does your family spend quality time? At a mall or at the kitchen table?

"Children entering adolescence acquire virtually boundless new opportunities for pleasure, power, and escape into illusion. So strong is the natural urge to

conform, and so powerfully seductive are the temptations
toward indulgence, that children simply must have a
powerful inner strength of will to resist. Peer pressures
are only permanently successful when they move into a
vacuum in the children's inner character."[6]

James B. Stenson

*Your children will imitate people
they admire. Is that you?*

The Pressure on You

The biggest pressure on you is to be the person your child emulates
and to be the kind of person your child hopes to be. This is your main
job.

Please don't let our culture place unyielding demands on you to
perform perfectly as a mother. I've tried to emphasize that you cannot
possibly do everything, nor can you do everything right. Please don't
drive yourself crazy trying to reach perfection for yourself or for your
children. Your children will not suffer permanent damage if they don't
get into the "right" preschool, summer camp, or college, if they are
denied the perks of affluent parents, or if they experience hardship
as a result of your circumstance. As one writer commented, "(The)
example of steadfast, heroic love can have a profound effect on the
children's moral makeup."[7] Frankly, they may grow all the better for
not having that "leg up" we so covet these days.

Parenting is give and take. Certainly, at times we have no options
and must abide by God's law. Much of the time we have latitude and
can sensibly implement new strategies without the old "Bible over the
head" routine. Keep in mind, however, that one generation's liberality
is the next generation's excess.

Pray for grace, Mom. Pray for the grace to stand firmly focused on
the Lord. Pray for grace to be able to communicate His way of life to
your children. Pray for grace to have patience without compromising
God's values. Pray for grace to keep your home holy. Display signs
and symbols of your covenant relationship with the Lord. Hang a

simple statement on your wall: "As for me and my house, we will serve the LORD" (Joshua 24:15).

Holidays

I felt it necessary to mention holidays in this chapter because of recent cultural trends. I have a few questions.

Family should be the primary peer group.

Does promoting the holiness of holidays ruin it for the kids? Why have we sold out to secular myth? Since when was Santa born of a virgin, and when did the Easter bunny die for our sins? How come Christmas vacation is now winter recess and Easter holiday spring break? Why do we allow our children to dress up as occultic figures on Halloween... in school, no less? Why is Thanksgiving a national day of football and beer, and the Fourth of July a day to party and get drunk? What's going on? The ways of the world are blindsiding us, and we are allowing it in the name of tolerance. I'm not promoting intolerance! Just watch out. Cultural trends deny any hint of the spiritual message of Christmas and Easter, and that is all the more reason for you to enforce it at home.

Celebrate holidays, but please, keep the holy ones holy. (You'll find holiday suggestions in chapter 12.)

_____ RESOURCES _____

Dr. Kathy Koch is founder and president of **Celebrate Kids.** Dr. Koch is a leading champion of children's worth and present value. Celebrate Kids offers a free e-newsletter. (www.celebratekids.com)

SADD (Students Against Destructive Decisions) is a group of students helping students make positive decisions about challenges in their everyday lives. From substance abuse to bullying to teen sex to alcohol, this is an excellent tool for teens dealing with peer pressure. It was founded as Students Against Drunk Driving. (www.saddonline.com)

Alcoholics Anonymous is a voluntary, worldwide fellowship of men and women from all walks of life who meet together to attain and maintain sobriety. (www.alcoholics-anonymous.org)

Al-Anon/Alateen. These programs are designed to help family members who are affected by alcoholism. (888-425-2666, www.al-anon.alateen.org)

Parents. The Anti-Drug is a new parenting site launched the National Drug Control Policy of the White House. The goal is to help parents learn better communication skills. A parenting tips newsletter is available to help prevent drug use. (www.theantidrug.com)

NoTobacco is an antismoking website for geared for teens (it's very cool) with links to other antitobacco sites. (www.notobacco.org)

Abstinence Educators' Network, Inc. offers a plethora of programs to support teens to avoid premarital sex. It includes a chat room. (members. tripod.com/abednet/LinksT.htm)

Kill Your TV provides statistics about intellectual, academic, psychological, and social effects of TV. (www2.localaccess.com/hardebeck/killtv2.htm)

Mediawise explains what media are doing to our children and youth and what we can do about it. (www.mediafamily.org/mediawise)

Family Safe Media lists many resources to help parental control over such things as TV, movies, the computer, and telephone. Includes valuable information on the V-chip to help you block and monitor television viewing, along with information on Internet filtering and tools. Highly recommended. (www.familysafemedia.com)

----------------- READING -----------------

James B. Stenson, *Preparing for Peer Pressure: A Guide for Parents of Young Children* (Princeton: Sceptor Publishers, 1988).

James B. Stenson, *Lifeline: The Religious Upbringing of Your Children* (Princeton: Sceptor Publishers, 1997).

Eleven

Safety

Crazed, fearless, and downright fierce when protecting our children, we women rise to the task with the powers of a superhero: Arnold Schwartzenmother. Pity the person who gets in our way. When protecting our young, mothers the world over can turn into prized pugilists, weight lifters, and emergency medical technicians in the blink of an eye.

Moms protect their kids not only from the threat of evil but also from an assortment of other issues: age-related fears, environmental safety issues at home and away from the house, traffic hazards, dangerous animals, weather-related danger, danger from terrorist attack, danger from food, danger from flood.

Regrettably, fear for personal safety is becoming a significant issue. Therefore, you must learn to protect yourself and your children by knowing how to identify and cope with conflict and threat. This chapter will help you prepare for emergencies that might come your way, encourage you to learn more, and prod you to take recommendations to heart and act upon them. As we have so tragically learned through terrorist attacks, school shootings, and severe weather incidents, preparation should be considered routine in every household.

Though it was long ago, I was once certified to teach basic first aid. I was also an Emergency Medical Technician and served as squad leader. During my time as an EMT, I responded to about 200 emergencies and continued my education through refresher courses and disaster simulation. As a girl I was a lifeguard and a Girl Scout. Most recently, I published a monthly newsletter called *Friendly Advice* in which I frequently wrote about safety issues. Some of that material is reprinted here.

Terror Emergencies and Disasters

The Department of Homeland Security posts a planning and prevention page on its website. It details three key steps that we all should take to be prepared for unexpected emergencies. I reprint the information here with some of my suggestions added. I urge you to take these recommendations seriously.

First, assemble an emergency kit. The Department of Homeland Security states we should be able to survive comfortably for at least a three-day period, which is the amount of time we may need to remain in our home until the danger of biological, chemical, or radiological attack has passed. For each person you will need these basics:

- a change of clothes
- sleeping bags
- a gallon of water per person per day and dried foods that are easy to store and prepare

Add basic emergency supplies to this kit: at least one good

flashlight, a battery-powered radio, extra batteries, a first aid kit, an extra set of car keys, prescription medicines and toilet articles, and duct tape and heavy-duty plastic garbage bags that you can use to seal windows and doors. Consider creating a separate kit for your car. This is vitally important, Mom, and you should act responsibly on this recommendation. Be sure that every family member knows where the emergency kit is.

Second, make a family communication plan.

- Your family may not be together at home when an attack occurs, so make sure everyone knows contact numbers and how to get in touch with each other. If cell coverage and phone coverage is not available, have repeated discussions about where you will all convene should something happen. Be certain the children understand that if separation is unavoidable they should remain calm and heed the supervision of other adults (such as teachers or babysitters) until you are reunited.

- Consider having everyone call an out-of-state friend or relative if you are unable to get through locally.

- Getting your teens to comply may be tricky, but nearly every expert in this field insists that every person carry some form of identification at all times. Sewing a name and address on a clothing label is a good start.

- Keep a list of emergency numbers near the phone.

- Select a "safe room" where everyone can gather in the house. The best choice is an inner room above ground with few windows and doors. (This may not be your best choice in some weather-related incidents.)

Third, learn as much as you can about readiness. Planning matters. If your family knows what to expect, they will be calmer in the aftermath of an event. For example, you should find out where to turn for instruction and how to access local broadcasting networks. Local authorities will broadcast information as quickly as possible concerning the nature of the emergency and what you should do next. Keep listening for updates and remain calm.

Here are some other ways to plan ahead. Take first aid and CPR classes so that you can provide emergency medical help. Review your insurance policies to reduce the impact of a potential disaster. Remember to make accommodations for elderly family members and neighbors or those with special needs. Also try to make arrangements for pets not allowed in public shelters.[1]

First Aid

A first aid kit and manual should be in every home and car. Dressings and bandages, adhesive tape, latex gloves, aspirin, syrup of ipecac (for poisoning), hydrogen peroxide, a snakebite kit, and antiseptic and ointments should be in the kit, as should extra prescriptions for any medical treatment necessary. I heartily recommend an old pair of eyeglasses as well, should you lose yours during an emergency, as well as hearing aid batteries, if needed. This kit should be readily available but off limits to little hands. I also advise you to keep a few extra gallons of household bleach someplace out of reach should the need arise to treat drinking water.

Emergency dressings can be fashioned out of sanitary napkins.

Water

The need to have water on hand is critical. Each time you are finished with a sturdy, closeable drink container, sterilize it, fill it with water, and put it in storage. If you know an emergency is coming, you may have time to fill containers, tubs, sinks, and pots and pans with water. Should you find yourself in dire need of water, you can tap an undamaged water heater, the tank of your toilet (not the bowl!), and even your water pipes.

If you need to treat water before drinking, the Federal Emergency Management Agency, known as FEMA, recommends boiling water for at least ten minutes and then straining. To each gallon add 16 drops of unscented chlorine bleach. Let the water stand for half an hour. If you can't boil the water, follow the protocol for the bleach. This will not eliminate all dangers from the water but should kill bacteria.

Other Items to Have on Hand

Do you have an extra stash of diapers? Formula? Pet food? Kitty litter? Safe candles and matches? What about scissors, a wrench to turn off utilities (and easily accessible notes to yourself on just how to do that), an ABC fire extinguisher, a tool kit, or a bathroom plunger? Try to think of each of the emergencies that might come your way and prepare for the needs of each family member. Don't forget to include diversions, such as cards or paper and pencils. Be prepared to evacuate, and know where your important papers are. Make certified copies of all important papers and keep a separate set in a safe-deposit box. Better yet, make two extra sets and secure one at the home of a trusted friend or relative.

Hard as this may seem, I recommend two more things:

1. Keep enough cash on hand to get you and the kids through a week or so. In some emergencies, ATMs and banks may not be available.

2. Keep your car's gas tank at least half-full at all times. From this moment on, Mom, I want you to slap your hand on your Bible and pledge that the half mark will always be considered empty. The time you need to make a quick getaway is not the time to need gas. It is also not the time to find yourself in a traffic jam. Think through routes you could take that might help you skirt congestion.

Family Drills

Include your older children when devising a family plan for every type of emergency that can come your way. Call the local fire department, police, and Red Cross or emergency responders and ask

e can come to your home to help your family devise
different emergencies. Though this is too serious
to be frivolous, younger children must not be scared witless. Part of
shielding them is enforcing their feeling of security and not creating
fearful or paranoid reactions. A little levity and gamesmanship should
be in order. Play make-believe with the children. Do this often.

- Make believe Mommy yells "Fire!" and tells you to get out of the house, or the smoke detector goes off.[2] Do you remember what the fireman told us when he/she came to our house? Where are you supposed to go? If Mommy isn't at the meeting place, where should you go next?

- Make believe Mommy tells you to call the police right away. What number do you call? If nobody answers when you call 911, you call 0, right? What is your name, address, and phone number? Extra hugs if you remember your county!

- Make believe you are at home with the babysitter and the weather gets very dangerous. Where do you go if there is a tornado? A hurricane? A flood?

- Make believe someone comes to the door or calls to you from outside and wants your help to find a puppy. Or wants to give you a treat and take you for a ride. Or tells you that Mommy is very sick or has gone away. What do you do? When you scream, "This is not my daddy (or mommy)!" and run away, where are you supposed to go?

- Make believe a bully threatens you on the playground. What should you say? What should you do? Whom should you go to?

- Make believe someone gives you a cigarette or alcohol or drugs. What do you say? Whom do you tell?

- Make believe you have to reach Mommy at work right away. How do you do that?

- Make believe someone touches you in your private area and tells you not to tell Mommy or he'll hurt you or get mad at you. What do you do?

- Make believe you are at a friend's house and he or she shows you a gun. What do you do? (Tragically, when I was an EMT one of my calls was to a home where a boy accidentally shot his brother in the face at point-blank range. I will never, ever forget the hysteria of the grandparents as they literally dragged me out of the ambulance when I arrived.)

- Make believe you encounter a strange dog, you get lost in a store, you fall in a swimming pool...on and on.

Fire Safety

- Invite a fireman to your home for evaluation and advice.

- Install smoke alarms. Some have built-in delays for the occasional burnt casserole. Fire departments often provide smoke alarms for free. Replace the battery on your smoke alarm annually.

- Don't put too heavy a load on one electrical outlet.

- Put safety caps on unused outlets that young fingers can reach.

- Don't exceed recommended wattage when you put bulbs in lamps.

- Turn off high-wattage lamps when not needed.

- Do not ever drape clothing or the like over lamps. This is an important tip to share with college students.

- Hellooo! Don't smoke.

- Do not wear loose clothing near flame of any kind, including a gas stove.

- Do not leave food unattended while it's cooking.

- Please be extra vigilant when using portable heaters. Read and follow the manufacturer's instruction.

- Kids and matches or lighters or candles do not mix.

- Do not even consider burning a candle in your home unless you are fiercely attentive. Ditto oil lamps.

- Please use extra care around the holidays. Dry trees, extension cords, lights, bayberry-scented candles, congestion, space heaters, excitement...you get the picture.

- If you store a nine-volt battery in the junk drawer, be certain to put it in an envelope or put tape over the terminals. A nine-volt has terminals on one side. If it connects with metal (such as a screwdriver, a flashlight, or paper clips) a house fire can result.

Protecting Yourself at Home

Post these National Domestic Violence Hotline numbers near your phone: 800-799-7233, TTY: 1-800-787-3224.

I have been abused. Some abuse was sexual, some was physical, some was emotional, some was mental. Some abuse happened to me when I was little, some happened to me as a teen, some happened to me as a young woman, and some when I was in my early thirties. I was abused when I could not defend myself, and I was abused when I had the autonomy to get away. Why I allowed abuse to happen when I was older is a mystery in spite of everything I've read.

I tell you this to let you know I totally understand that you may have allowed abuse to happen to you too. I also tell you this to tell you to get away if abuse is still occurring. Look under Crisis Intervention in your Yellow Pages for a number you can call. Protect yourself and protect your children. Here are some other practical measures you can take to protect yourself from harm:

- Change locks on your home.

- Be absolutely certain that every accessible window and door is locked before you leave your home and before you go to bed at night.

- Keep an outside light on at night.

- If at all possible, get a dog. Not some yippy little thing…get a dog that has enough loyalty and power to take out anyone threatening you but that will not harm a fly under any other circumstance. A growl or a threatening bark might be just enough to let a predator know the dog means business.

- Make sure one of your rooms can be considered a "safe room" with a strong lock, and if you have to sequester yourself, try to bring a cell phone with you.

- Do not answer surveys over the phone. Hang up when telephone solicitors call. Best yet, get caller ID so you know who is calling and can be selective with your response.

- Install a peephole in your door and a security chain on it. Do not open your door just because someone rings the bell. If someone needs help, get information through your locked door and place a call on his or her behalf.

- Ask for a photo ID of anyone who claims to be a sales or service person. If you have doubts, phone the company for verification. This applies when you are in a motel room and someone claims to be staff and wants access. Call the front desk to confirm.

- Neither you nor your children should ever give the impression that you are home alone.

- Do not be quick to give personal information to strangers regardless of how safe they might seem. Predators don't show up in red suits with long tails and pitchforks. They are usually smooth operators, some work in teams, and some teammates are women.

- If foliage is blocking the front of your home, knock it down and plant daffodils. (Thorny bushes directly against the house are deterrents.) Invite the local police to visit your home and assess it for areas where someone could lurk.

- Get some pepper spray if young children can't get their hands on it and if it is legal in your state and municipality.

- Do not keep a gun in the house. Kids can be Harry Houdini himself if they set their minds to getting into something.

- Take a self-defense class. These are often offered by the local police department.

Protecting Yourself on the Street

- Try to know your route well—where you can run for help as well as areas where someone could be hiding.

- Wear shoes and clothes that will not hinder escape.

- Try not to walk alone, especially at night or in poorly lighted areas.

- Walk against the direction of traffic. Someone will be less likely to pull you into a car.

- Walk confidently. Act as if you know what you're doing. Attackers choose people who look vulnerable.

- Walk away from doorways, alleys, and bushes. Keep toward the street side of the sidewalk.

- If you think someone is following you, cross the street or change directions. Go into a busy place. Don't go home! The last thing you want is for someone to know where you live.

- Avoid people who are loitering.

- If possible, don't carry a purse. If you do, carry one with a long sturdy strap and sling it over your head onto your opposite shoulder. Try to get along with a fanny pack.

- If you have a purse and someone grabs it, let it go. (This is a really good reason to photocopy your license, credit cards, and insurance cards and to keep a few copies at home or in a safe-deposit box.)

- If you carry a lot of packages at once, you will appear vulnerable.

- Do not give the "correct time" if asked, do not read while waiting for the bus or metro, do not flash money in public, and do not be distracted while talking on a cell phone.

- Carry a whistle and don't be afraid to use it.
- If someone is threatening you, make a scene and fight for your life. If he succeeds in getting you off to a deserted place, the fight will be much harder—with more predictable results.
- Experts say you shouldn't call, "Help!" because not everyone responds. Yell, "Fire!" loudly.

What to Do in Case of Rape or Attack

- No single strategy works 100 percent of the time. You must use your judgment.
- Stay as calm as possible. Sometimes pushing in toward your attacker can throw him off guard. This may give you a split second of looser grip in order to wriggle out and flee.
- You will have to decide if submitting is more advisable than resisting.
- These are some of your options: nonresistance, negotiation, stalling, distracting the assailant, verbal assertiveness, screaming, and physical resistance. (Please consider taking a self-defense course!)
- Remain alert and observant so you can describe everything to the police.
- Fight like the dickens to stay out of a car. If you are driving, crash into something in a very public area if possible. Try to keep the crash to a minimum to avoid severe injury.

Protecting Your Children from Kidnapping

- Drill, drill, drill about strangers, straying from your eyesight, and warning signs.

- Make sure your children understand that they are not to believe anyone who tells them that something has happened to you and that they must go with that person, even if it is the father (unless the father is one of the designated caregivers on your list).

- Make sure they know how to use a telephone in case they must contact the police or call you at work or at home.

- Be certain they are in the care of protective adults or older siblings at all times.

- Be certain that all caregivers for your children have seen a copy of your custody agreement and that they understand your children are not to be taken from their premises by anyone but you or the people you designate. Be firm about this.

Caregiver Instructions

If your children are in the customary care of someone, have a notarized medical release in that person's possession and at your child's doctor's office should you trust the judgment of that caregiver.

As I mentioned previously, *What to Expect Baby-Sitter's Handbook* is a must resource for every home.[3] Within this handbook are many lists for you to complete that give instructions for everything from the child's sleeping patterns and favorite foods to contact numbers and your instructions about what to do in an emergency. This is also an excellent resource for you as the mother because it covers many possible scenarios and will help you to keep a clear head should something happen. It is a terrific bedside book that you should consult regularly just to keep refreshed.

Safety in Your Car

- Make sure child seats and seatbelts for all others are installed properly. I once responded to an accident when a baby went through a car window like a football.

- Keep your car in good working order.

- Park in well-lighted parking lots that are easily accessible. Park on the ground level to avoid stairways and elevators.

- Carry a small flashlight and check the backseat of your car before entering.

- Don't be a pattern parker, even at work. Vary your routine so you don't become an easy target.

- Have your keys ready as you approach your car. When you enter, lock your car at once.

- Never get into a car with a driver who has been drinking. Most drunk driving accidents happen in the late evening or early morning and on weekends.

- Never pick up a hitchhiker or stop to help someone who is stranded. Use your cell phone to inform authorities and do what I do: Pray the Lord will send a carload of people to help.

- Keep your windows rolled up, and always keep your car locked. Always.

- Keep your purse out of sight. Put belongings in the trunk or keep them concealed.

- At stoplights, leave space between you and the car in front of you—don't box yourself in. Stop in the center lane when possible to avoid potential offenders.

- Do not travel unfamiliar routes at night.

- Do not leave your car if you are bumped from behind or someone says your tire is flat. Drive to a well-lighted service station or the local police department. Once you leave your car you are open for attack.

- If you have a flat in a remote or scary place, listen to your instinct—ruin the tire, ruin the rim, but continue to drive (slowly) to the nearest source of help.

- Chill out if someone is riding your bumper—let the person pass. Road rage is everywhere. Don't encourage it. That also means no gestures or scowls when the person does pass, and no eye contact. Never get into a car with an assailant—it is the worst possible situation. Do anything to avoid it. Run, fight, and scream.

- Stay up to date on the criminal activity in your community.
- Do not go to ATM machines in the dark or even in the daylight if no other people are nearby.

Teen Driving

Teen driving fatalities are heartbreaking situations for many families. Consider enforcing the following rules to prevent this from happening to your family:

- Postpone your teen from getting a license for as long as possible.
- Insist that your teen take driver's education in school.
- Spend a lot of time with your teen driving and observe his or her driving habits. You should be the one to decide whether your child is mature enough and experienced enough to handle a car.
- No friends in the car when your teen is driving. Period. No exceptions. (In some states, this is a law for kids of certain ages.)
- Expect your teen to pay for the extra cost of insurance.
- Think twice before you allow your teen to get a car, especially if car payments are involved.
- Only allow your teen to drive to places you've driven to together.
- Don't put your teen behind the wheel of a powerful or sexy car.
- Encourage everyone in your family to take public transportation, ride a bike, or walk.

—————————— READING ——————————

Talking About Disaster: Guide for Standardized Messages provides the latest, most up-to-date information on disaster preparedness and safety in the United States. This guide provides standardized safety messages on 19 natural, technological, and human-induced hazards, as well as general disaster preparedness and safety topics. It is available from the website of the National Disaster Education Coalition. (www. disastereducation.org)

Brent Q. Hafen and Keith J. Karren, *First Aid and Emergency Care Workbook Manual* (Englewood, CO: Morton Publishing, 1990).

Twelve

Having Fun Through It All

It's time we had a little fun...especially after that cheerful last chapter! My goal in this chapter is to offer affordable and fun ideas for the family.

Play is the child's world, and children learn about the world through play. Whether your baby is grabbing at a colorful mobile in a crib, your three-year-old is holding his own in a raucous playgroup, your 11-year-old is exploring every nook and cranny of a hiking trail, or your teen is strategizing over the next move during a game of chess, life skills abound when children play. Make-believe was a big part of emergency preparedness for good reason—children's imaginations often soar much higher than ours.

We all played once. As a mother you no doubt find yourself in the middle of play, marching single file through the house, dancing to music with the kids, laughing over a board game, or playing touch football in the backyard. You feel better after you've played, don't you? Red nosed from an afternoon of sledding, breathless after a game of catch (you didn't want to keep those fingernails long, anyway), sore and dusty after hiking a five-mile loop, crusted with sand after a day at the beach. Play brings a bonus: It is fun to plan, fun to do, and fun in the aftermath. We all need more play.

Some Fun Ideas:

- Make a miniature golf course in your living room. Use boxes, mugs, boards, books. Get creative! Use an upside-down umbrella as a putter.

- Blow soap bubbles.

- Go on a nature safari and collect bugs.

- Make a lemonade stand.

- Make a homemade band with pot tops, coffee cans, wooden spoons, and beans in a tight Tupperware container.

- Make puppets from socks, gloves, or mittens and put on a show. The use of puppets can be invaluable in getting children to express their inner feelings.

- Create a masterpiece out of macaroni, bottle caps, pieces of fabric, old greeting cards. Use Elmer's glue.

- Go to the park. Many municipal parks have a duck pond. I don't know of too many kids who don't like to feed ducks.

- Go to the zoo or to a petting zoo. It would be super if you could develop a relationship with a farmer who would welcome you all for a visit.

- Climb to see a pretty view. Go early in the morning to watch the daybreak and bring a breakfast picnic. Do this before work and school.

- Create a family newsletter or cookbook.
- Buy an inexpensive plastic kiddie pool and a couple bags of sand. Put the sand in the pool, hand over some old plastic bowls, cups, big spoons, an old pot or two, and turn the young ones loose.

Winter Activities

- Track down a long-lost relative.
- Go to an indoor driving range or swimming pool. Join the Y.
- Label all your family tapes and DVDs.
- Read a novel. Better yet, have your children read it to you.
- Pick a theme and become budding photographers. Find barns or fire stations or people wearing red or brown dogs or birds...
- Write and perform a comedy act.
- Gather all your loose photos and put them in a scrapbook or photo album.
- Make something like a bird feeder together. Paint your broom handle wacky colors. Paint the handles of lots of brooms and sell them at a flea market.
- Frame a picture. Get creative.

Keep a family fun to-do list in a prominent place and keep it doable.

Rainy Day Kid Stuff

- Invent a new soup together. Get bold with herbs and spices.
- If your child is old enough and you supervise, carve a bar of soap. Start with something easy, like the Leaning Tower of Pisa. Learn about it in an encyclopedia or on the Net and then make pizza.
- Write a story. Invent characters with funny names. Turn it into a mystery.
- Sort through all the children's belongings and prepare for a kids'-only yard sale.

- Buy a sack of hard candy and go visit a nursing home.
- Build a fort by draping blankets and sheets over furniture. Have a picnic inside the fort.
- Make a list of things to find inside the house and then go on a searching safari.
- Play a board game. Invent a board game.
- Go to the library.
- Airports can be lots of fun to explore.

Diversions

- Encourage hobbies. Explain to the kids what a hobby is and help them identify what would appeal to their orientation and talents.
- Encourage interest in collecting. Stamps, old bottles, baseball cards...the sky is the limit.
- Encourage sports. Many fabulous sports can build confidence in a child. If you can, install an outdoor basketball hoop.
- Hiking as a family can bring great pleasure and reward.
- Bring your home into the woods or alongside a lake—go camping. An air mattress and a few blankets will do if you don't have much money. Pack peanut butter sandwiches for breakfast. Bring lemon essential oil to keep the skeeters away.
- Try to pick toys that provide fun and function for your child, with some emphasis on learning skills.
- Promote the arts. Keep lots of paper in the house and have watercolors available. Ask the kids to design place mats for the table. Keep a special bulletin board for projects the kids produce in school. (The fridge is too "same old.")
- Set up a table in a corner of a room and start a puzzle that is not too hard for your children to complete.
- Put in a family garden. Give each kid a pack of seeds and the

responsibility for that particular crop. Have a family fair at the end of season; invite relatives and friends and award ribbons.

Entertaining Ideas

- Invite people over for a "come as you are" party.
- Or an upside-down party (breakfast for dinner).
- Or an inside-out party (clothes inside out, shoes on wrong feet).
- Or a pajama party.
- Or a leftover party (everyone grabs what's in the fridge and convenes at one person's house).
- Announce to your children's friends that you are hosting a "special day" party for your child—just because. Instead of presents, each guest shares one sentence explaining why that child is special. (If you do this for one, be certain to do it for the other children in the family.)
- Host a breakfast. Hosting a breakfast party has many advantages:

  1. It's fun! Weather permitting, hold the breakfast outside. The more rugged the better. Build a campfire and spread a table with goodies.

  2. It's frugal! Breakfast is an inexpensive way to feed friends. French toast, juice, chunks of fresh fruit, and hot chocolate would do. You could add scrambled eggs, a few quick breads with an assortment of toppings, or breakfast sausages. Precut everything and it will serve more.

  3. It's different! People are different in the morning.

  4. It's inclusive! Children and dogs make the event complete.

  5. It's tidy! Everyone helps clean up...and then they all leave. You have the rest of the day to yourself.

> *Always have an announced alternative plan in case Dad does not honor a commitment to show up.*

Too

...need downtime and you need playtime. Being with the kids 24/7 is hard for anyone. You must have adult companionship, conversation, and camaraderie, or you'll go bonkers. (That would not be good for the kids.) The chapter on leaning on others stressed this.

Some of you have built-in downtime because the children are with their father for routine visitation. Some of you do not have this arrangement, or the father is gone. Turn to your network and find reliable care for your children so you can have an occasional weekend to yourself. Then go someplace. Try to do this at least quarterly if you can afford the expense. Preferably, go someplace with a friend. Here are some ideas:

- Go on a church retreat. They're inexpensive, and you might enjoy super food, nourishment of soul, and perhaps new friends who share your circumstance. If your church isn't planning a retreat, find a church that is. Scholarships are often available for those who cannot afford the fee.

- Travel someplace off-season for low rates. The benefit is low crowds. The disadvantage is usually poor weather, but at least you did something.

- Go to the next town and explore. Spend the night at a moderately priced chain motel. (Some "inexpensive motels" aren't what they seem to be!) If you go with friends, you can split the cost.

- Colleges and organizations often offer tours.

- Volunteer to chaperone a group, to usher at a concert, or to help at a special function.

- Do you have a friend or relative who would offer you their spare room in another town?

- If you can afford a trip, all-female getaways are quite popular. Check with AdventureWomen for active trips for women over 30. (800-804-8686, adventurewomen.com.) Also check with the Women's

Travel Club to inquire about their many yearly trips. (800-480-4448, womenstravelclub.com)

Holidays

If your loss is fresh, any holiday can be tough, with birthdays and anniversary dates probably competing for the top spot. I urge you to seek counsel if you find yourself slipping into depression triggered by special days. Keep your memories alive, by all means, but for your sake and the sake of your children, make new ones. If you are having a particularly hard go during a holiday or remembrance, establish a ritual that might help you to cope.

- Write a birthday card or anniversary card to your husband and tell him how much you miss him. Keep the card in a beautiful box—or burn it outside on a clear night. Offer it up to God.

- Plant a tree on a day that brings sorrow to you.

- Immerse yourself in the service of others during the hard times.

- Create a new holiday tradition. If you are widowed, hang on to those traditions that honor your husband.

The Holidays Alone

This wasn't the "alone" time you had in mind, was it? The kids are with their father eating turkey and pumpkin pie, and you're in front of the tube with Lean Cuisine.

Coping through holidays alone is not good for anyone—and we all know what happened to Scrooge when he cloistered himself! Make it top priority to find someone to share holidays with. If you have no one, volunteer at a shelter, nursing home, or hospital. Somebody else needs cheer more than you do.

Everyone is stressed during holidays, especially at Christmas. Add the difficulty of your circumstance and perhaps some tense moments

:x and his family, and stress can escalate to full-fledged war. ...edge now to keep Christmas, in particular, holy, simple, and peaceful.

Your children may struggle as they bounce around and invariably find themselves in the company of strangers if they visit their dad. Make this as easy on them as you can. That might mean buttoning your lip. If the father has remarried, his wife may be on tilt, trying to impress your children that she is not the evil stepmother. She is most likely trying to garner some sort of respect for her position in their lives. The children must be top priority during this time.

Mother's Day and Father's Day

If your children are small, you may have to help them create a Mother's Day masterpiece for you. Ditto Christmas present. It is perfectly okay for you to help them to "surprise" you. Don't deny them this.

Father's Day can be a conundrum. There is more to this day than meets the eye. I see three different situations here:

1. Kids in school.
2. Kids who love their dad.
3. Kids who couldn't care less about their dad.

Kids in School

What to do about the preschooler or the kindergartner who makes a Father's Day gift in school? I have a couple of ideas. If the child has a male role model, a beloved grandfather or uncle, or even a much older brother, the gift can be channeled there. The child can also offer his or her gift to someone in a nursing home or at the Veteran's home. I recommend you read from the Bible about God as Father, however, and encourage the child to present that gift to God. This may help establish a child-father relationship on a spiritual level. Simply visit a church and place the gift on the altar. They won't mind.

Kids Who Love Their Dad

You may not, but they do. This cannot be discouraged, regardless of your relationship or history with the father. Father's Day must be considered equally with other holidays for the sake of your children. For children whose father has died, this is an extremely difficult time. I urge you to find ways to help them express their love for their departed dad. A visit to the cemetery may mark this annual celebration. Don't deny your children their grief. Talk to them and share the wonderful memories they hold for their father.

Kids Who Couldn't Care Less About Their Dad

This is not unusual. There may be a range of emotions behind some children's seeming disregard for this holiday. Those emotions have got to be addressed—wise counsel is recommended. However, some children simply do not relate to their father. In that case, Father's Day has no meaning to them and should not be pushed.

Holidays Suggestions

- Plan to keep things peaceful and work to keep them simple.
- Nothing is wrong with separate children's seating for casual dinners when others come by with their kids, but children should celebrate holidays at the same table as adults.
- Pick out a Family Festival Day to celebrate each year. Give thanksgiving to the Lord for your very unique and special family.
- Make banners for your home to celebrate all the Bible festivals of the year. This is an excellent opportunity for the family to creatively learn about the Bible.
- Celebrate fall instead of Halloween. Instead of carving gruesome

faces on a pumpkin, make pumpkin people, drawing faces on pumpkins and stuffing old clothes.

- Find a local church that has a creative alternative for Halloween, such as an indoor carnival.
- Put up a yule log and advent candles.
- Put up a crèche and read the Christmas story.
- Teach giving instead of receiving. For years Joe and I gave our two nieces splendidly wrapped empty boxes, representing money spent not on them but on someone less fortunate.
- Speaking of gifts…

A Gift to You

I hope my gift to you in this book has been hope and confidence. I hope with all of my heart that this gift made today a bit easier and encouraged you to live your life well. I felt it fitting to end this book with words of encouragement from some of the many single mothers I spoke with for this project.[1]

"Being single means you have fear and frustration, but ultimately you have to believe in yourself. You may hurt, you may be in pain, but it gets better day by day. You have to give your will to God—it took me to be at my boiling point. I know I have to trust Him. That's where I am today. I trust God. I died to me years ago, and I know that because He lives I can do one more day. Come out of your pity room and go into your waiting room. It's not easy. I'm not going to lie to you." (Bonita)

"You cope one day at a time. You need the confidence to know that you can take care of yourself and your kids. You need to know that bullying on his part cannot disempower you from doing what's right. You need money and the means to continue a good income. You need friends, love, support, and fun because you face fears, failure, and loneliness. Your challenge is to balance your life and your children's. You must learn to manage time and money. If you are depressed, get help." (Sheila)

"God is our Father and provider. He created the family unit, not single parenthood. Whatever the circumstances that have put someone into this position, we must lean on Him to supply our every need, praying for wisdom to discern what is a legitimate need and allowing Him to provide it. It is a challenge, but it can be done!" (Andy)

"Single moms are no different from married moms in what we want for our children. We all want the best for our children when it comes to education, friends, opportunities in life. We have a lot of the same fears. Fears for their safety, media influences, too much television, are they getting enough vitamins, fruits, and vegetables.

"But as single moms we also worry that our kids are shortchanged by not having two parents. Are we bringing our daughters up to not trust men because of our own insecurities and past hurts? We face the fear of not having enough money in a single-income household. How are we to balance work, school, and family. Is it okay to date? Am I selfish to crave companionship, love, and security? Do I take the chance of someone else walking out of their lives or not date and take the chance of not meeting someone who would be a good male role model and father figure? Mostly, are we teaching our children not to trust or rely on anyone because as single moms we usually only have ourselves to depend on? It is important for children to learn independence, but not to the point that they can't open up to other people.

"You just have to put it in God's hands, which sounds easier than it is. No matter how strong your faith is, sometimes letting go of the worry is the hardest part. Pray for guidance and keep the lines of communication open and never start the day or go to bed at night without giving your kids a hug and telling them you love them." (Shane)

"You cannot do it without knowing the power of God. Even if you do know the Lord there are times you are desperately tired and lonely. And that's where you will make poor decisions if you don't have God and good friends. I only want what we need. It is a day by day struggle. I am always glad when I go to bed at night and have made it through one more day!" (Jennifer)

Live well!

_____ *Soli Deo Gloria* _____

Notes

Chapter 1—The Many Faces of Single Mothers

1. "Growth in Single Fathers Outpaces Growth in Single Mothers, Census Bureau Reports," U.S. Census Bureau. (www.census.gov/Press-Release/cb98-228.html)

2. Source: U.S. Census Bureau. Cited in "Facts About Single Parent Families," by Parents Without Partners International, Inc. (www.geocities.com/pwp_winnipeg/facts.htm)

3. Abigail Trafford, "Grandparents Help Define Family Values, My Time," *The Washington Post*, February 28, 2005.

4. An AP article titled "Army Seeks to Save Marriages Torn Apart by War" cites studies showing divorce rates as high as 21 percent when one spouse has been sent to war. *Daily Inter Lake*, December 30, 2004, p. A10.

Chapter 2—Coping

1. Rob Stein, "Laugher's Link to Health May Be in the Blood," *The Washington Post*, March 14, 2005, p. A10.

2. Cited in Malcolm Gladwell, "The Eyes Have It," *Reader's Digest*, February 2005, pp. 129-33.

3. "Arun Gandhi's Very Positive Approach," *The Washington Post*, March 2, 2005, p. C3.

4. R.K. Harrison, ed., *Encyclopedia of Biblical and Christian Ethics* (Nashville: Thomas Nelson Publishers, 1992), s.v. "Forgiveness."

5. Tracy Grant, "Mother, Don't Apologize; Just Embrace the Guilt," *The Washington Post*, February 28, 2005, p. C11.

6. Carl Pickhardt, "December 2002 Psychological Update: Divorce and the Season for Forgiveness." (www.carlpickhardt.com) Dr. Pickhardt is a well-published author and psychologist in Austin, Texas. He offers monthly online articles about parenting.

7. Dan Schaefer and Christine Lyons, *How to Tell the Children* (New York: Newmarket Press, 1986).

8. John and Paula Sandford, *Transformation of the Inner Man* (Tulsa: Victory House Publishing, 1982).

9. Carl Pickhardt, "March 2003 Psychological Update: Strengths of the Single Parent." Used by permission. (www.carlpickhardt.com)

Chapter 3—Leaning on Others

1. "Do not take advantage of a widow or an orphan. If you do and they cry out to me, I will certainly hear their cry. My anger will be aroused."

2. Quoted in Constance M. Green, "One House, Two Single Moms," *The Washington Post,* April 5, 2005, p. C9.

3. Quoted in D'Vera Cohn, "4% of U.S. Homes Are Multigenerational; Culture, Finances Dictate Lifestyles," *The Washington Post,* September 7, 2001, p. A8.

4. Ibid.

5. Quoted in G. Jeffrey MacDonald, "Single Parents Learn Hope," *USA Today,* November 3, 2004, p. 6D.

6. Quoted in "Fatherhood Activists Protest TV Commercial Mocking Dad," *USA Today,* November 10, 2004. (www.usatoday.com/news/nation/2004-11-10-fathers-protest_x .htm)

7. Amy Dickinson, "Ask Amy," *The Chicago Tribune,* February 17, 2005.

8. R.K. Harrison, ed., *Encyclopedia of Biblical and Christian Ethics,* (Nashville: Thomas Nelson Publishers, 1992), p. 250.

Chapter 4—Leaning on the Lord

1. Charles F. Pfeiefer and Everett F. Harrison, eds., *The Wycliffe Bible Commentary* (Chicago: Moody Press, 1962), p. 938, and R.K. Harrison, ed., *Encyclopedia of Biblical and Christian Ethics* (Nashville: Thomas Nelson Publishers, 1992), p.114, conclude that in this teaching Jesus was looking at the hardness of men's hearts and their casual attitude toward divorce. This passage is intended to protect wives from husband's whims.

2. Jeanne Marie Laskas, "News You Can't Lose," *The Washington Post Magazine,* March 6, 2005.

3. "Should Parents Make Kids Attend Religious Services?" *Parade Magazine,* December 8, 2002, p. 26.

Chapter 5—Finding Time for It All

1. Eleanor Berman, *The Cooperating Family* (Englewood Cliff, NJ: Prentice-Hall, 1977), p. 19.

Chapter 6—Affording It All

1. Much of the material in this chapter was previously published in my book *Money and Me: A Woman's Guide to Financial Confidence,* currently out of print.

2. Throw away all catalogs when they come. Better yet, take your name off the mailing lists. For a five-dollar fee, you can decrease the junk mail you receive by writing to Mail Preference Service, c/o Direct Marketing Association, P.O. Box 9008, Farmington NY 11735-9008, or visiting (www.dmaconsumers.org/cgi/offmailinglist).

3. Quoted in Mindy Fetterman, "Parents: Money Training Works," *USA Today,* October 29, 2004, p. 2B.

4. From "The Financial Expert" column, *Money Magazine,* April 2005, p. 56B.

Chapter 7—Staying Healthy Through It All

1. Julie Appleby, "Health Care Tab Ready to Explode," *USA Today,* February 24, 2005.

2. "One-Third of Kids Destined to Be Diabetic," *USA Today,* June 14, 2003.

3. Mary Beth Janssen, *Radiant Beauty* (Emmaus, PA: Rodale Press, 2001), p 24.

4. Simone Kosog, "Silence in the Monastery," in Peter Seewald, ed., *Wisdom from the Monastery* (Old Saybrook, CT: Konecky & Konecky, 2003), p. 318.

5. Kate Barnes, *How It Works: The Human Body* (London: Award Books, 1996).

6. The pancreas produces insulin. Carbohydrates spike our need for insulin. Slow-absorbing carbohydrates put less stress on the pancreas. If overstressed, the pancreas may become exhausted, and type 2 diabetes may follow. "Even without diabetes high insulin levels are undesirable because they increase the risk of heart disease." Jennie Brand-Miller, et al., *The Glucose Revolution* (New York: Marlowe & Company, 1996), p. 4.

7. Joseph Mercola, "Why the U.S. Is Developing More Exercise Deficiency Syndrome." (www.mercola.com/2005/jan/5/exercise_deficiency.htm)

8. Sari Harrar, ed., *The Sugar Solution* (Emmaus, PA: Rodale Press, 2004), p. 90.

9. Marilynn Marchione, "Too Little Sleep Raises the Risk of Being Overweight," reprinted in the *Daily Inter Lake,* November 17, 2004, p. A18.

10. Timothy Jordan, *Food Fights and Bedtime Battles* (New York: Berkley Trade, 2001).

11. Quoted in "One-Third of Kids Destined to Be Diabetic," *USA Today,* June 14, 2003.

12. Harrar, *The Sugar Solution,* p. 90.

13. "U.S. Children Under 10 May Have Diabetes," *New England Journal of Medicine,* March 14, 2002.

14. Sally Fallon, *Nourishing Traditions* (Winona Lake, IN: New Trends Publishing, 1999.)

15. Mary Enig and Sally Fallon, *Eat Fat, Lose Fat* (New York: Hudson Street Press 2004).

16. These ingredients were listed for General Mills' Reese's Puffs, with such claims on the box as "Strong Bones!" and "Goodness Corner."

17. These ingredients were listed for General Mills' Wheaties, which claims on its box it is "fitness fuel."

18. Fifty-six percent of eight-year-olds drink soda every day, and the average teenage boy drinks three cans of pop each day. In 2000, 15 billion gallons of pop were sold. Can somebody tell me why we don't give our children water any more? No, not water with chemical flavorings added…just good, filtered, water.

19. Fallon, *Nourishing Traditions,* p. 24.

20. David K. Shipler, "Children Going Hungry," *The Washington Post,* February 27, 2005.

21. Eric Scholsser, *Fast Food Nation* (New York: Perennial, 2002).

Chapter 8—Child Care

1. Heidi Murkoff, *What to Expect Baby-Sitter's Handbook* (New York: Workman Publishing, 2003)

2. "Child Care—Finding High-Quality Care." (www.aap.org/pubed/ZZZ3IIGC44D. htm?&sub_cat=13)

3. Mary Eberstadt, *Home Alone America* (New York: Penguin, 2004).

4. Kristyn Kusek, "They're Home, You're Not...Now What?" *Readers Digest,* February 2005, pp. 140-45.

5. "Kids Busy with Out-of-School Activities," *Daily Inter Lake,* November 16, 2004.

6. "Life Is Sure Busy—for Kids." (www.publicagenda.org/press/clips/all_work_no_play_clip_cnn.pdf)

Chapter 9—Discipline Through Discipling

1. George Will, "'Therapism' Is No Substitute for Stoicism," *Daily Inter Lake,* April 21, 2005, p. A4.

2. J. Grant Howard, *Balancing Life's Demands* (Portland, OR: Multnomah Press, 1983), pp. 92, 95.

3. James B. Stenson, *Lifeline: The Religious Upbringing of Your Children* (Princeton, NJ: Scepter Publishers, 1997), p. 1.

Chapter 10—Cultural Bombardment and Peer Pressure

1. "Is TV Morphing Your Child nto a Bully?" *Archives of Pediatrics & Adolescent Medicine,* April 2005, 384-88. (archpedi.ama-assn.org/cgi/content/short/159/4/384)

2. Carl Pickhardt, "November 2004 Psychological Update: Electronic Brain Training and ADD/ADHD." (www.carlpickhardt.com/pages/484148/index.htm)

3. Peg Tyre, Julie Scelfo, and Barbara Kantrowitz, "The Power of NO," *Newsweek,* November 13, 2004, p. 45.

4. Courtland Milloy, "Selling Sneakers by Violating Young Minds," *The Washington Post,* March 2, 2005.

5. James B. Stenson, *Preparing for Peer Pressure: A Guide for Parents of Young Children* (Princeton, NJ: Sceptor Publishers, 1988), p. 35.

6. Ibid., pp. 14-15.

7. Ibid., p. 45.

Chapter 11—Safety

1. "Three Key Steps That Individuals and Families Should Take to Be Properly Prepared for Unexpected Emergencies," U.S. Department of Homeland Security. (www.dhs.gov/dhspublic/interapp/editorial/editorial_0287.xml)

2. Some smoke detectors can be programmed with your voice rather than a loud noise. Children may react better if they are awakened from sound sleep by their mother's voice giving them directions.

3. Heidi Murkoff, *What to Expect Baby-Sitter's Handbook* (New York: Workman Publishing, 2003).

Chapter 12—Having Fun Through It All

1. Of interest for this model is that single mothers were selected at random. I did not require that they be women of faith. Their answers almost universally point to a relational need for God.